Racing
MASERATIS

GIANCARLO REGGIANI

Racing
MASERATIS

Giorgio Nada Editore s.r.l.

Editorial manager:
Luciano Greggio

Art editor:
Aimone Bolliger

Colour photographs:
Giancarlo Reggiani (Harald Blondiau - 300S)

Black and white photographs:
Maserati Archives; A. Sorlini, E. Ferraris - Giorgio Nada Editore Archives

English translation:
Robert Newman

Cover design:
Sergio Nada

Editorial office:
Luca Banchio

Thanks for their kind co-operation go to:
Antonio Alberoni, Giancarlo Casoli, Ermanno Cozza, Mario Galbiati, Matteo Panini, Roberto and Lorenzo Sommi, Giuseppe Tommasetti, Gianni Torelli, Giovanni Vitali.

Special thanks and appreciation go to Luigi Orsini and Franco Zagari, authors of 'Maserati: a Story Within a Story', published by Emmeti Grafica for the Libreria dell'Automobile of Milan.

Giorgio Nada Editore
Via Claudio Treves, 15/17
I – 20090 VIMODRONE (Milano)
Tel. +39 02 27301126
Fax +39 02 27301454
E-mail: info@giorgionadaeditore.it
www.giorgionadaeditore.it

The catalogue of Giorgio Nada Editore publications is available on request at the above address.

Racing Maseratis - ISBN: 88-7911-252-X

CONTENTS

This book is a brief study of some of the most important Maserati racing cars ever built. It ranges from the pre-Second World War 6CM to the short-lived 420M "Eldorado" and the glorious 250F; from the legendary A6GCS that wrote pages of the company's sports car racing history, to the 1992 Barchetta via the 150S and the 200SI. Here, we have brought together just a few important contributors to the outstanding sporting history of Maserati: an assembly that is the result of pains-taking research into cars which, today, have been perfectly conserved or restored, and are, beyond question, in their completely original form. Not many Maserati racing cars have remained in Italy and, worse still, investigation has confirmed there are no examples of the 450S at all in its homeland, a car that almost managed to capture the world constructors' championship for its manufacturer in 1957. The logic behind the selection of cars for this book led to the discovery of some extremely rare Maseratis, which have been well conserved or restored. In the chapters that comprise this lingering look at some of the most beautiful and successful cars of their time, priority has been given to spectacular colour pictures of these magnificent machines in their current splendour, but without forgetting the need to show them in action with pictures from the past and, naturally, an accurate historical and technical description of all the cars featured here.

Giancarlo Reggiani

6CM

(1936-1939)

"**V**oiturette" was an affectionate sobriquet for the diminutive 1500 cc single-seaters of the Thirties, in contrast to the more powerful and imposing Grand Prix cars of superior formula, but in reality the name did little justice to the actual performance of these cars, which had a top speed of around 143 mph. One of the most successful Maseratis of the period, the 6CM, brought honour to its category, with its maximum power output of 155 hp at 6200 rpm, which climbed to 175 hp with the updated final version of the series. Always looking for economic stability, Maserati production erred on the side of cars with good sales prospects, partly ignoring the more demanding world of Grand Prix cars. The presence of the "voiturette" certainly met this need, in that their reasonable price brought sales success and a healthy profit for the company. Maserati produced 27 6CMs, 19 of which were sold and eight became works cars: for the period, those figures were equal to a low volume production run. The 6CM, a natural evolution of the illustrious 4CM, was in reality a derivation of the earlier, more powerful Grand Prix Maserati, the V8 RI, with its supercharged engine that developed 320 hp at 5300 rpm. From its predecessor, the 6CM took its chassis of longitudinal and transverse members and, in part, the rounded appearance of its aluminium body, which also resembled the last generation of the 4CM. The 6CM had a six-cylinder in-line, 1493 cc engine with twin overhead camshafts and Roots supercharger. Unlike the 4CM, the car had innovative independent front suspension with torsion bar and friction dampers; its rear axle remained rigid, with semi-elliptic springs. The car was 25 hp more powerful than the first version of the 4CM, but its weight

continued on page 11

continued from page 8

increased to 650 kg against the 580 kg of the older car. The speed of the 6CM left its predecessor standing though: 143 mph against 118 mph of the first 1932 version of the 4CM 1500. The 6CM made its track debut part-way through the 1936 racing season and immediately singled itself out from its opponents for its notable potential, returning good results in its class in a number of races. The car also had the honour of being the first Maserati to go on display at a motor show, in Milan in October 1936: on the stand at which the House of the Trident began its presence at the great shows, the 6CM was offered for sale at Lit 95,000 (about 6700 US $), a highly competitive price that brought it within the reach of many. It almost seemed as if the car could not get enough of the spotlight: it went on to

continued on page 13

◁
◁
◁ *An aggressive yet elegant profile: the 6CM expresses its vocation for speed, emphasised by the long line of air vents on the bonnet, and its exhaust.*

▽
▽ *The extraordinary symmetry of a number of features renders this picture almost abstract: the two mirrors become simple lights and the steering wheel assumes a graphic dominance.*

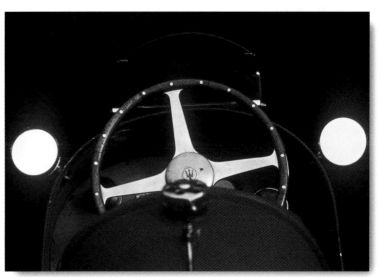

▷ The characteristic Maserati radiator grill almost seems to be imprisoned in the slender front of the 6CM single-seater. The central hole below the grill is for the car's starting handle.

△ The original circular holes in
this patented Maserati fuel
filler cap acted as vents for
the fuel when it reached too
high a pressure while racing.
Worked by a spring, a special
membrane inside the cap
only allowed a small amount
of fuel to seep out.

continued from page 11

dominate its class on the Italian stage throughout 1937,
and was justly rewarded with the country's 1500 title, driv-
en by Ettore Bianco; this most 'ambitious' of single-seaters
continued to win a long series of races, in which it was
campaigned by some of the top drivers of the period. The
6CM triumphed at the Grand Prix of Tripoli, where it took
the first five places in the 1500 cc class driven by René
Dreyfus, Franco Cortese, Francesco Severi, Luigi Villoresi
and Piero Dusio: the car went on to win the Circuit of
Naples driven by Carlo Felice Trossi, the Coppa Acerbo
with Giovanni Rocco, the Circuit of San Remo driven by
Achille Varzi, the Circuit of Lucca with Trossi again and the
Grand Prix of Brno driven by a star of the future, Gigi
Villoresi. In that same year, the unresolved financial difficul-

continued on page 16

◁ The cockpit was dominated by
the huge, wood-rimmed
steering wheel.

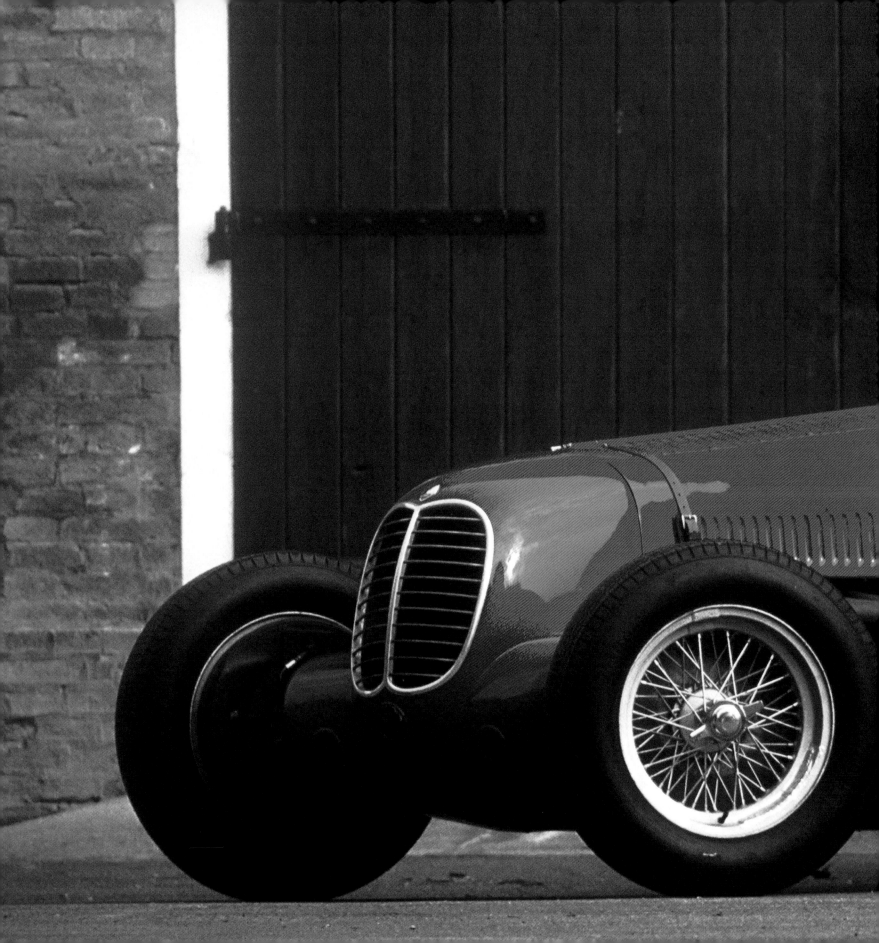

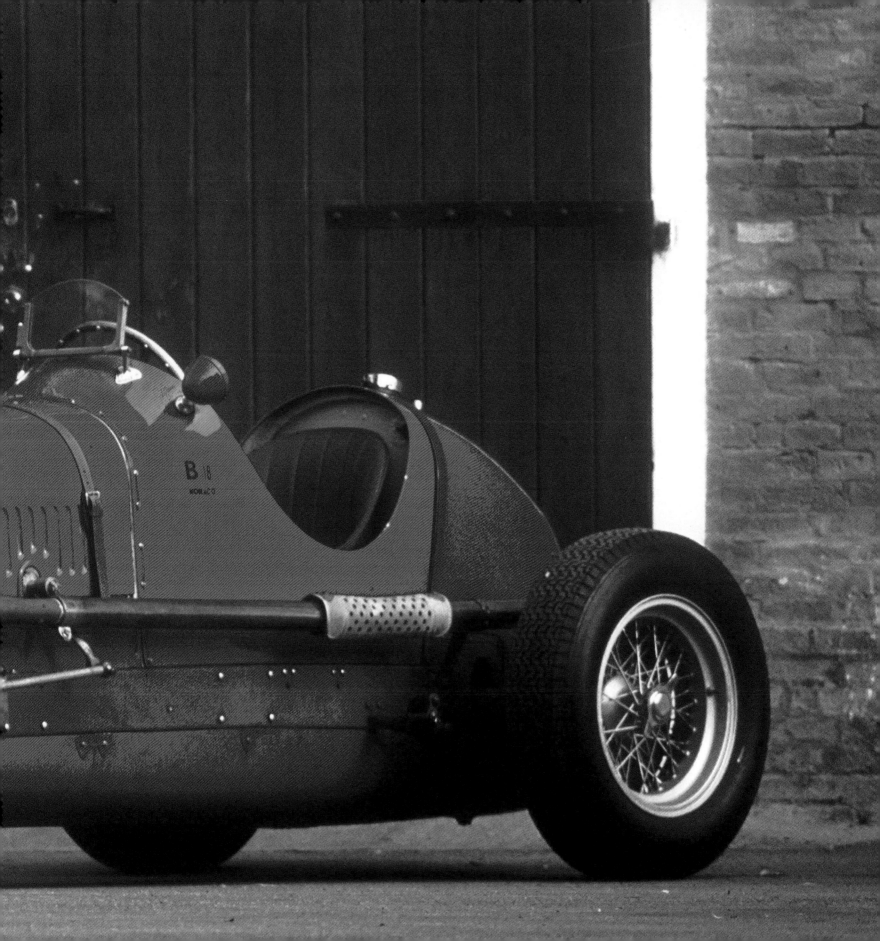

continued from page 13

ties of the Maserati brothers lead to the acquisition of their company by the Orsi brothers, already owners of several factories in the iron and steel industry. After the change of hands, the new order of the day meant, not surprisingly, that Maserati production was transferred from the brothers' hometown of Bologna to the Orsi's operational centre at Via Ciro Menotti, Modena, where it remains to this day. The sale relieved the Maserati brothers, who remained with the company by special agreement, of the not inconsiderable task of managing the business they had built from nothing and gave them the opportunity to concentrate with greater serenity exclusively on their projects and the development of their magical machines. A point of interest is that, before being pensioned off in 1940, the ex-Piero Taruffi 6CM was used as a 'driving school car' by a young hopeful named Alberto Ascari: at Tripoli, the Milan driver came ninth in the car. As well as playing an important role in the promotion of the Maserati name in the world of motor racing, the 6CM left its creators with an important inheritance: its engine and other components were used for the development of the A6, the first sports tourer built by Maserati to race in the sport car class.

▷ *In line with the times, the tail was of a much-tapered design, typical of the fashionable pointed shape of the day. It was only in later years that designers learnt the advantageous secrets of the stubby rear-end.*

▽ *To the left of the driver's seat is the protection sleeve fitted to the exhaust pipe at the level of the driver's arm: its purpose was to stop him from burning himself on the hot exhaust pipe.*

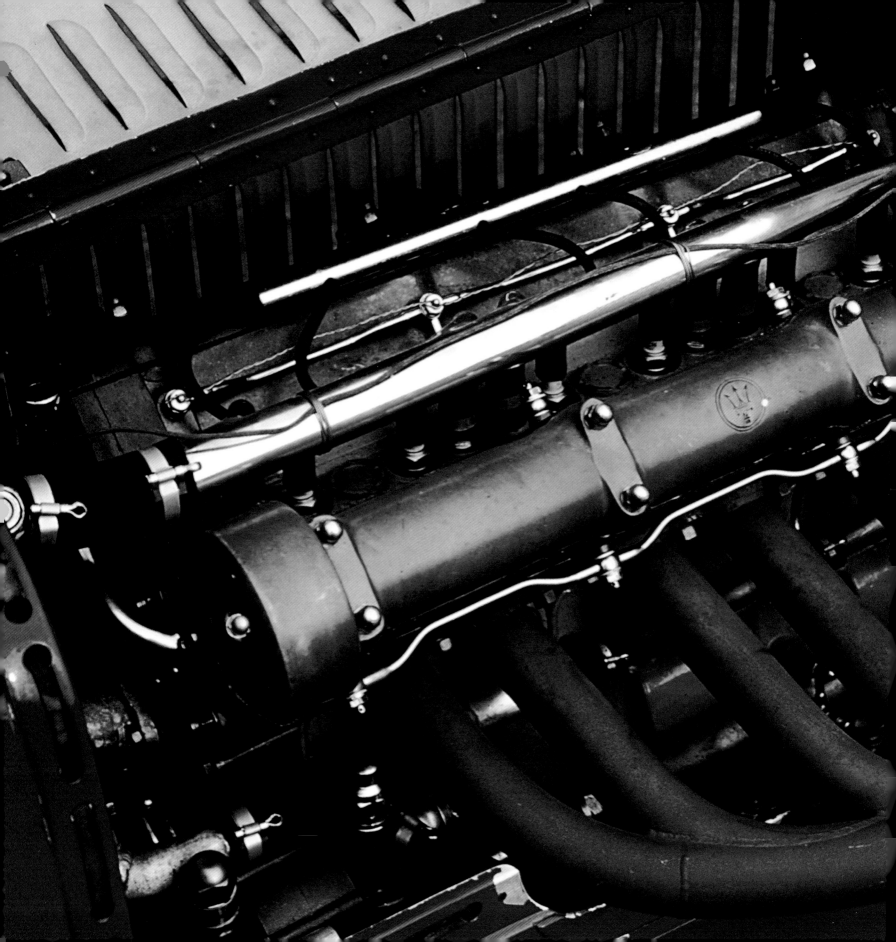

Technical specifications

ENGINE

Front, longitudinal, six cylinders in line
Bore and stroke: 65x75 mm
Cubic capacity: 1493.2 cc
Valve gear: twin overhead camshafts driven by gears
Number of valves: two per cylinder
Compression ratio: 6:1
Fuel feed: one Weber 55AS1 (55-50DCO) carburettor on a
              Roots supercharger
Ignition: single, with magneto
Cooling: water
Lubrication: dry sump
Maximum power: 155-175 hp at 6200-6600 rpm

TRANSMISSION

Rear wheel drive
Clutch: single dry disc
Gears: four forward speeds plus reverse
Gear ratios: -
Axle ratio: 10/48

BODY

Single-seater, in aluminium

CHASSIS AND MECHANICS

Chassis: longitudinal and transverse members
Suspension: front - independent, torsion bars and friction dampers; rear –
              rigid live axle, semi-cantilevered leaf springs and friction
              dampers
Brakes: hydraulically operated drums front and rear
Steering: worm and sector
Fuel tank: 122 litre capacity
Wheels: spoked, 4.00x16, 4.00x17
Tyres: front 6.00x16 – 5.25x17; rear 6.00x16 – 5.25x17

DIMENSIONS AND WEIGHT

Wheelbase: 2490 mm
Track, front: 1200 mm
Track, rear: 1200 mm
Length: 3720 mm
Width: 1480 mm
Height: 1200 mm
Weight: 650 kg

PERFORMANCE

Maximum speed: 143 mph

△ Water temperature and oil pressure are indicated by these two instruments with different coloured dials.

◁◁ The pedal arrangement was unusual: they were placed either side of the transmission. The clutch is on the left, the rectangular accelerator in the centre and the footbrake on the right. To change gear, drivers had to reach down between the four spokes of the big wood-rimmed steering wheel for the gear lever.

▽ The black dialled tachometer, the 6CM's most important instrument, stands out on the right of the dashboard and is of much larger diameter than the other dials.

Chassis and engine numbers

Engine 1530 *(1936)*: Hans Ruesch, Zurich, Switzerland
Chassis and engine 1531 *(1936)*: Gino Rovere, Turin
Chassis and engine 1532 *(1936)*: Maserati works car
Engine 1533 *(1936)*: Luciano Uboldi, Roncate, Switzerland
Chassis and engine 1534 *(1936)*: Moris Bergamini, Mantua
Chassis an engine 1535 (1936): Frank McEvoy, Australia
Chassis and engine 1537 *(1936)*: Maserati works car shown at the Milan Motor Show and then sold in 1937 to Austin Dobson, Great Britain
Chassis and engine 1538 *(1937)*: Austin Dobson, Great Britain
Chassis and engine 1539 *(1937)*: Gino Rovere, Turin
Chassis and engine 1540 *(1937)*: Giovanni Rocco, Naples
Chassis and engine 1541 *(1937)*: Luigi Villoresi, Milan
Chassis and engine 1542 *(1937)*: Franco Cortese, Milan
Chassis and engine 1543 *(1937)*: Maserati works car, later sold to Ettore Bianco, Genoa
Chassis and engine 1544 *(1937)*: Maserati works car
Chassis and engine 1545 *(1937)*: Fritz Gollin, Erfurt, Germany
Chassis and engine 1546 *(1937)*: J. Peter Wakefield, Great Britain
Chassis and engine 1547 *(1937)*: Austin Dobson, Great Britain
Chassis and engine 1548 *(1937)*: Herbert Berg, Altena, Germany
Chassis and engine 1551 *(1937)*: the Earl Howe, Great Britain
Chassis 1552, engine 1551 *(1938)*: Cotton Henning, USA
Engine 1553 *(1939)*: Maserati works
Chassis 1554, engine 1550 *(1938)*: Eugenio Minetti, Scuderia Ambrosiano, Milan
Chassis 1556, engine 1555 *(1938)*: Georges Raph, Paris
Chassis 1557, engine 1556 *(1938)*: Maserati works car for Carlo Felice Trossi, Aldo Marazza, Mario Mazzacurati
Chassis 1558, engine 1557 *(1938)*: Eugenio Minetti, Scuderia Ambrosiana, Milan
Chassis 1560, engine 1559 *(1938)*: Maserati works car for Giovanni Rocco, Franco Cortese, Paul Pietsch, Luigi Villoresi
Chassis 1561, engine 1660 *(1937)*: Arialdo Ruggeri, Gallarate
Chassis 1562, engine 1561 *(1938)*; Maserati works car for Luigi Villoresi
Chassis 1563, engine 1562 *(1938)*: Maserati works car for Luigi Villoresi
Chassis 1565, engine 1565 *(1939)*: for Giovanni Rocco and Paul Pietsch

▽ 26 September 1937: Luigi
Villoresi winning the Circuit of
Masaryk at Brno,
Czechoslovakia, in the
Maserati 6CM.

▽ *22 May 1938: Giovanni Rocco on his way to winning the XXIX Targa Florio in a Maserati 6CM.*

A6G.CS "Monofaro"

(1947-1953)

Alfieri, six-cylinder, Ghisa, Corsa, Sport: it was with the first letter of each of those words that this fascinatingly malevolent-looking Maserati barchetta was baptised. Words that seem less mysterious and technological than the initials by which this motor racing legend is known. On their own, the letters and number six seem almost indecipherable, but they perfectly define the personality of the car, and, as desired by the owner of the factory at the time, Ernesto Maserati, also pay tribute to the memory of the man who founded the company but who died prematurely, Alfieri Maserati. The G indicated that the engine's block was in ghisa, Italian for cast iron, and Corsa in Italian means racing, so A6G.CS.

The first public appearance of this Maserati took place in 1947, when double world champion to be Alberto Ascari and seasoned veteran Luigi Villoresi began to test drive the barchetta, its body in plain sheet aluminium with motorcycle-style mudguards, in September on the mountainous roads of Abetone, Italy, between Modena and Pistoia. From the centre of the classic double ellipse radiator grill jutted a large headlight, which earned the Maserati its diminutive of Monofaro or Single Headlight from enthusiasts and the company's employees alike.

The body of the car was built by the Medardo Fantuzzi coach builder of Modena, as were most of the other A6G.CS models that followed: a company that was able to shape the elegant sporting image of Maserati barchettas with great style.

The engine, a six cylinder in-line 1978.7 cc transplanted directly from the A6 sports tourer, was given an increase in power to produce 130 hp at 6000 rpm, against the original

continued on page 27

continued from page 24

65 hp at 4700 rpm of its donor. One weak point about the mechanics of the A6G.CS Monofaro was its gearbox, which was not exactly built for racing, as it was the same as the one fitted to the Fiat 514 normal production car: used on the much more demanding Maserati sports car, the box created reliability problems. The compression ratio of the six-cylinder Maserati was notable, at 11:1, demanding the use of a fuel mixture with a base of methyl alcohol. These were the technical features of the racer with which Maserati planned to compete in the sports car category and take on tough opponents like Cisitalia, Gordini and Talbot, as well as its nearby rival down the road at Maranello, Ferrari. The appearance of the A6G.CS Monofaro was vaguely similar to that of the car of the Prancing Horse against which it would have to go into combat: the 125 S. Both were virtually open wheelers, wearing only small motorcycle-type mudguards and both were of similar dimensions and shape. But in 1947, an "aerodynamic" version of the 125 S was also produced with covered wheels, a feature that did not appear on the Maserati until the last few examples of the A6G.CS were built. The car was the work of Engineer Alberto Massimino, the man who later designed perhaps the most famous Ferrari, the 250 Testarossa, the chassis of which was based on the traditional concept of a structure in ellip-

◁ *Maserati's worn Trident logo can still be made out on the cast clutch and brake pedals of the A6G.CS.*

▷ *The headlamp set into the radiator grill and the motorcycle-type mudguards give the Monofaro its unmistakable personality.*

 tically-sectioned Mannesmann steel tubing without welding, and the adoption of the semi-elliptic spring suspension for the rear axle. Just 16 of these cars were built, of which at least three had an integrated body with wings and a closed bodyshell. Of these, number 2003 was a coupé, 2019 and 2039 were open top bodies in aluminium by Guglielmo Carraroli with wings incorporated; one became a works car, another was bought by the Automobile Club of Brazil and the third by Maserati's U.S. importer, Antonio Pompeo.

The first series of the A6G.CS achieved some success in motor racing, although it also had to retire on numerous occasions due to banal reliability problems. But the car got off to a convincing start by scoring a 1-2 first time out: driven by future Formula One World Champion Alberto Ascari, Monofaro number 24 won the Circuit of Modena on the 28

continued on page 32

△ *The Monofaro's aluminium dashboard stands out: to the right of the driving position, the large, Jaeger rev counter that reaches 6000 rpm. In the centre is the oil pressure gauge with the Trident logo prominent on its white face.*

▷ *The traffic indicators on the front mudguards have a vaguely aerodynamic design, typical of the end of the Forties.*

◁ The A6G.CS' motorcycle-type mudguards were widely adopted in Italy and overseas for the sports cars of the period.

▽ The long bonnet had two narrow air intakes: one above the radiator grill to feed the carburettors, and the other almost at the base of the windscreen to scoop up fresh air and channel it to the lower part of the cockpit.

continued from page 28

September 1947, with its sister car, driven by Luigi Villoresi, taking second place, thereby clearly declaring to its future adversaries that it was a car of tremendous potential. There was another 1-2 success in 1948, when the colourful but fast Giovanni Bracco won that year's Coppa D'Oro delle Dolomiti in an A6G.CS, with Luigi Villoresi once again second in another Monofaro. On 15 August that year, Alberto Ascari drove the single headlamp Maserati to victory in the Circuit of Pescara, after quite a battle.

The A6G.CS was one of the least expensive racing cars for private drivers of the period, as it cost less than Lit 4 million (about 13500 US $) and was competitive in both national and international events.

◁ Three Weber 36DO4 carburettors fed the six-cylinder in-line 1978.7 cc engine and the car's maximum power output was 130 hp at 6000 rpm.

△ The exit of the long exhaust pipe from the wing of a closed-bodied Monofaro: the car's spoked front wheels were fitted with either 5.50x15 or 5.50x16 tyres.

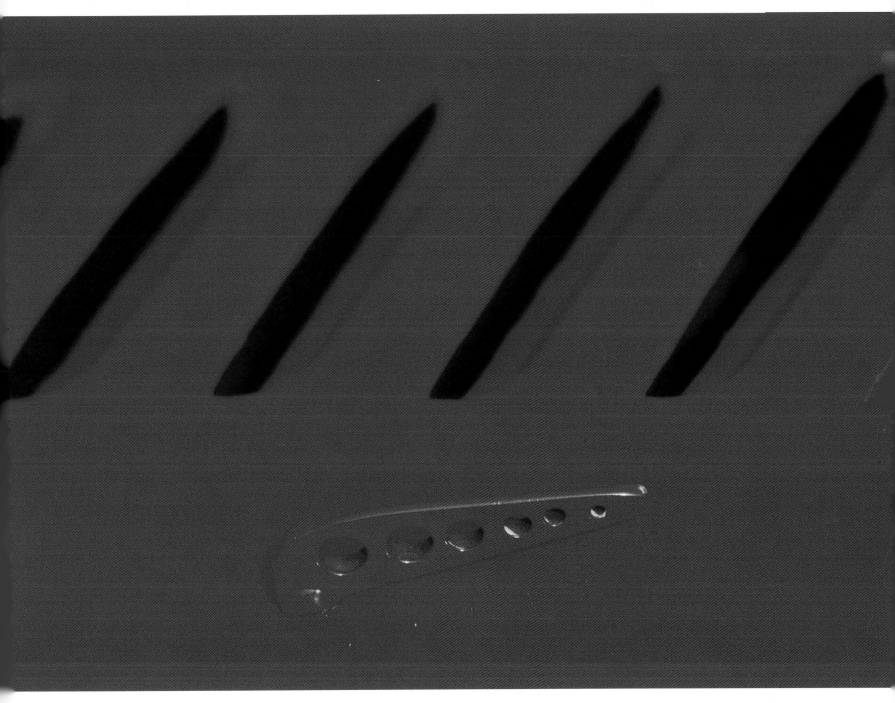

△ Bonnet air vents, under which
is a perforated aluminium
hood locking handle,
designed to minimise
aerodynamic resistance.

Technical specifications

ENGINE

Front, longitudinal, six cylinders in line
Bore and stroke: 72x81 mm
Cubic capacity: 1978.7 cc
Valve gear: single overhead camshaft driven by triple chain
Number of valves: two per cylinder
Compression ratio: 11:1
Fuel feed: three Weber 36DO4 carburettors
Ignition: single, with distributor
Cooling: water
Lubrication: dry sump
Maximum power: 130 hp at 6000 rpm

TRANSMISSION

Rear wheel drive
Clutch: single dry disc
Gears: four forward speeds plus reverse
Gear ratios: I) 3.68:1; II) 1.78:1; III) 1.35:1; IV) 1:1; R) 6.25:1
Axle ratio: 9/38

CAR BODY

Two-seater roadster, in aluminium

CHASSIS AND MECHANICS

Chassis: framework in elliptical-section tubes
Suspension: front – independent, upper and lower wishbones, helicoidal
springs and Houdaille hydraulic dampers; rear – rigid live
axle, longitudinal leaf springs, Houdaille hydraulic dampers
Brakes: hydraulically-operated drums front and rear
Steering: worm and sector
Fuel tank: capacity 100 litres
Wheels: spoked, 3.50x15 – 3.50x16
Tyres: front 5.50x15 – 5.50x16; rear 5.50x15

DIMENSIONS AND WEIGHT

Wheelbase: 2310 mm
Track, front: 1210 mm
Track, rear: 1150 mm
Length: 3690 mm
Width: 1380 mm
Height: 900 mm
Weight: 672 kg

PERFORMANCE

Maximum speed: 118-127 mph

△ The narrow, Spartan cockpit
of the A6G.CS is coherent
with a car that has a racing
destiny. Note the sparse
instrumentation and the large
diameter steering wheel.

▷▷ The large headlight of the first model of the
A6G.CS, set into the centre of the radiator grill.

△ The semi-elliptic spring
mount of the rear axle and
the attachment of the wing to
the body.

Chassis and engine numbers

Chassis and engine 2001 *(1947)*: Maserati works car
Chassis and engine 2002 *(1947)*: Maserati works car
Chassis and engine 2003 *(1947)*: Maserati works car with coupe body
Chassis and engine 2004 *(1948)*: Guerrino Faccioni, Vicenza
Chassis and engine 2005 *(1948)*: Vincenzo Auricchio, Cremona
Chassis and engine 2006 *(1949)*: Nicola Musmeci, Catania
Chassis and engine 2007 *(1948)*: Maserati works car, re-numbered
in 1949 as chassis number 2010
Chassis and engine 2008 *(1949)*: Guglielmo Dei, Rome
Chassis and engine 2009 *(1949)*: Emilio Romano, Brescia
Chassis and engine 2010 *(1949)*: Vianini, Argentina.
Chassis and engine ex-2007
Chassis and engine 2011 *(1949)*: Sonio Coletti Perucca, Rome
Chassis and engine 2012 *(1950)*: Autoclub do Brasil, Rio de Janeiro
Chassis and engine 2014 *(1950)*: Pietro Palmieri, Rome
Chassis and engine 2016 *(1950)*: Giovanni Bracco, Biella
Chassis and engine 2019 *(1952)*: Autoclub do Brasil, Rio de Janeiro
Chassis and engine 2039 *(1953)*: Antonio Pompeo, U.S.A., for display
at the Sports Car Show of New York

◁ 15 August 1948: the two Maserati A6G.CS numbers 10 and 8 in the pits were soon to become leading players at Pescara, driven by Alberto Ascari. The Milan ace started in number 10 but was forced to retire with mechanical problems. In the pits, he took over Giovanni Bracco's number 8 car and won the race. Second was A6G.CS number 7, driven by Luigi Villoresi.

A6GCS/53

(1953-1955)

A harmony of curves and tapering lines, one of the most elegant vehicles that ever raced on four wheels. The A6GCS barchetta, its body designed by Medardo Fantuzzi of Modena is, without doubt, one of the most attractive sports cars to have graced the red-hot asphalt of motor racing. To keep up with its competitors, Maserati took the decision in 1953 to graft a much more streamlined and aerodynamic body onto the chassis of the A6GCS first series, a design with the exclusive purpose of bettering the car's performance on the long, fast straights of the mid-Fifties' road races. But aesthetic-cum-aerodynamic modifications were not the only improvements made to the car: to have a realistic chance of challenging its opponents, the Maserati's mechanics had to be updated, especially the engine.

That was how the six-cylinder in line, which had already been installed in chassis 2019 and 2039 of the first series, came to be fitted to the new car, but this time with its cubic capacity increased slightly to 1985.6 cc, twin overhead camshafts and double ignition. The compression ratio was reduced from the original, high 11:1 to 8.75:1, which produced more vigorous traction and made the car easier to drive; the power output of the second series, which some also called the A6GCS'53 or Sport 2000, was also increased, to 170 hp at 7300 rpm.

Maserati's new barchetta immediately appealed to its customers and the car's sales success was memorable. Between 1953 and 1955, 52 units were produced, the last of which – chassis number 2099 – became a prototype of the 300S.

continued on page 45

◁ The large tachometer with its blue face, calibrated to 8,600 rpm. The manufacturer's logo appears on the Maserati Register badge on the right.

▽ A detail of the rear wing shows the able work of the panel beater in shaping the somewhat aerodynamic tail of the A6GCS.

continued from page 42

Most of the second series bodies were built by Medardo Fantuzzi, although specials were also produced by Fiandri, Frua, Scaglietti, Vignale and even Pininfarina, which designed and built four outstanding sports tourers, the subject of the next chapter, on chassis numbers 2056, 2057, 2059 and 2060. Number 2042, built in 1953 for Sergio Mantovani of Milan, was by Sergio Scaglietti and looked similar to the Ferrari barchettas, which Scaglietti also fashioned.

The body built in 1953 by Vignale on chassis number 2049 was, certainly, one of the most non-conformist A6GCS barchettas, with a concave chrome "mouth", a rounded and decisive body shape, unique flowing lines, a winged profile that developed itself along the flanks and the contours of the boot, with longitudinal relief to simulate a streamlined head rest which was, in fact, non-existent: without doubt, all of those features combined to make the car a stylistic masterpiece of great impact. It was bought by the American Tony Parravano, but was re-bodied by Sergio Scaglietti in 1955.

continued on page 48

continued from page 45

But most A6GCSs were of the Fantuzzi stamp, so they were only different from each other in detail: for example, some had a radiator grill that accommodated two deeply sunken headlights, others had vertical grill bars and no Maserati trident; others still had a large central trident and horizontal bars.

Additional distinguishing details that often set one example apart from another included the shape of the plexiglas windscreen, and the presence or absence of a supplementary air intake on the bonnet. But one constant feature was the fitment of two large Marchal headlights, which were always there on the front end of the A6GCS.

continued on page 53

▷▷ *The A6GCS was fitted with 4.50x16 spoked wheels and 6.00x16 cross ply tyres, although this example wears Pirelli's more modern Cinturato CF67 radial.*

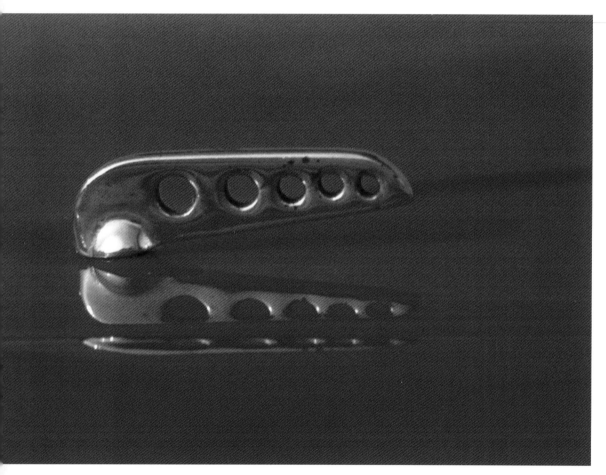

△ *As with most racing cars of the period, the bonnet opening lever was perforated for lightness with holes of diminishing diameter.*

▽ In the Spartan yet functional cockpit, the two bucket seats, with their efficient side supports, are separated by a large transmission tunnel. The tubular structure of the chassis can be seen on the inside of the doors, making access rather difficult. The pale blue dials stand out on the car's dashboard, and a stubby gearlever of pure motor racing heritage is slotted into the H-shaped selector grill.

△ Some examples of the A6GCS/53 were given slightly concave radiator grills, with three horizontal bars and a large Trident logo in red.

continued from page 48

The motor sport pedigree of this Maserati is impressive: the car scored significant victories, winning its class in the 1953 Mille Miglia, coming second and third in 1954 fourth overall and first in class in 1955. The second series A6GCS continued to race until 1957, winning Britain's Tourist Trophy, Italy's Coppa delle Dolomiti, the 1953 Italian Sports Car Championship and the 2000 cc class of the same championship in 1954. And Spanish nobleman Alfonso De Portago, who acquired A6GCS chassis number 2076 direct from the factory, made his motor racing debut in the car.

▽ Double exhaust pipe terminals, set into a special housing under the left side of the car, is one of the distinctive elements of the A6GCS/53.

△ The lightness and equilibrated shape of the front and rear wings are emphasised by how perfectly they blend with the line of the flanks.

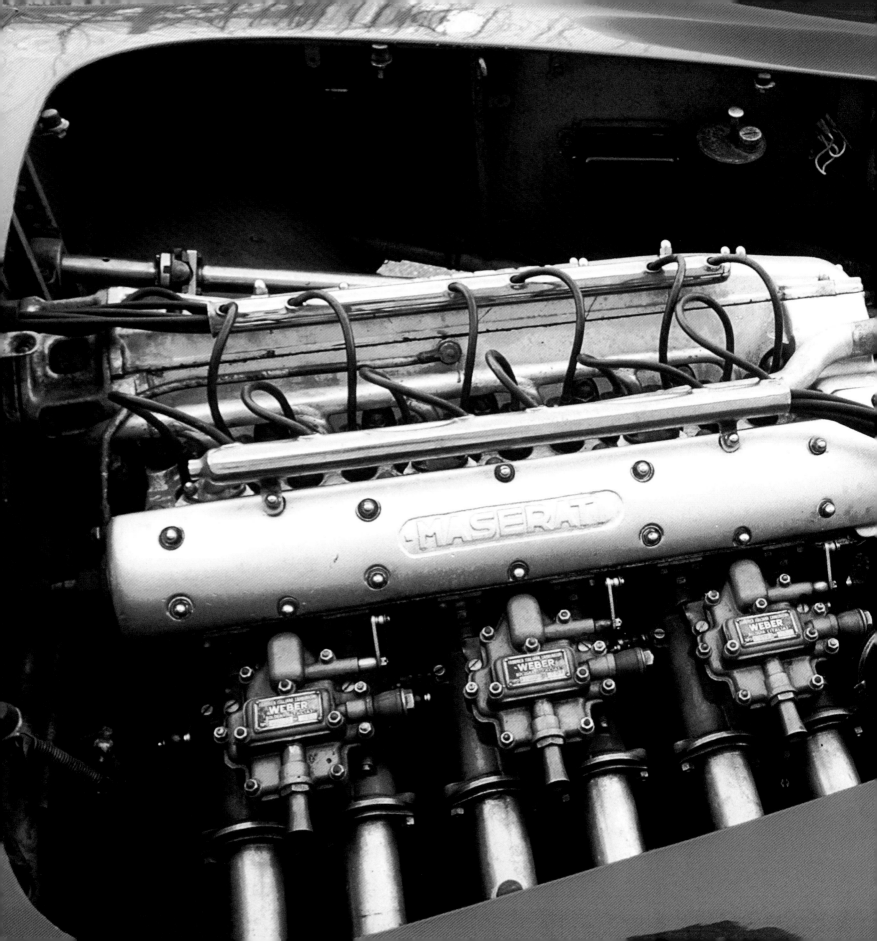

Technical specifications

ENGINE

Front, longitudinal, six cylinders in line
Bore and stroke: 76.5x72 mm
Cubic capacity: 1985.6 cc
Valve gear: twin overhead camshafts driven by gears
Number of valves: two per cylinder
Compression ratio: 8.75:1
Fuel feed: three Weber 40DCO3 carburettors
Ignition: double, with magnetos or distributors
Cooling: water
Lubrication: dry sump
Maximum power: 170 hp at 7300 rpm

TRANSMISSION

Rear wheel drive
Clutch: dry multi-disc
Gearbox: four forward speeds plus reverse
Gear ratios: I) 0.452:1; II) 0.715:1; III) 0.847:1; IV) 1:1;
       R) 0.284:1
Axle ratio: 8/40

BODY

Two-seater roadster, in aluminium

CHASSIS AND MECHANICS

Chassis: framework in elliptical-section tubes
Suspension: front – independent, upper and lower
      wishbones, coil springs and Houdaille
      hydraulic dampers; rear – rigid live axle, longitudinal
      semi-elliptic springs and Houdaille hydraulic dampers
Brakes: hydraulically operated drums front and rear
Steering: worm and sector
Fuel tank: capacity 125 litres
Wheels: spoked, 4.50x16
Tyres: 6.00x16

DIMENSIONS AND WEIGHT

Wheelbase: 2310 mm
Track, front: 1335 mm
Track, rear: 1220 mm
Length: 3840 mm
Width: 1530 mm
Height: 860 mm
Dry weight: 740 kg

PERFORMANCE

Maximum speed: 146 mph

Chassis and engine numbers

Chassis and engine 2040 *(1953)*: Emilio Giletti, Biella
Chassis and engine 2042 *(1953)*: Sergio Mantovani, Milan
Chassis and engine 2043 *(1953)*: Luigi Musso, Rome
Chassis and engine 2045 *(1953)*: Gianni Restelli, Milan
Chassis and engine 2047 *(1953)*: Guglielmo Dei, Rome
Chassis and engine 2049 *(1953)*: Tony Parravano, USA
Chassis and engine 2050 *(1953)*: Gianni Bertoni, Ferrara
Chassis and engine 2052 *(1953)*: Gilby Engineering, Great Britain
Chassis and engine 2053 *(1953)*: Ducati Motors, USA
Chassis and engine 2054 *(1953)*: Guglielmo Dei, Rome
Chassis and engine 2055 *(1954)*: Ducati Motors, USA,
for display in New York
Chassis and engine 2056 *(1954)*: Guglielmo Dei, Rome,
for Count Gravina
Chassis and engine 2057 *(1954)*: Guglielmo Dei, Rome,
for Pietro Palmieri
Chassis 2058 and chassis 2058 *(1954)*: Ducati Motors, USA
Chassis and engine 2059 *(1954)*: sports tourer for the Paris Motor Show
Chassis and engine 2060 *(1954)*: Guglielmo Dei, Rome
Chassis and engine 2061 *(1954)*: Maserati works car
Chassis and engine 2062 *(1954)*: Carlos Tomasi, Argentina

▷ *The original concave area at the base of the wing brings a little more élan to the rear end.*

▷ *Identification plaques bearing the car's engine and chassis numbers are part of the fascination of this works Maserati A6GCS/53.*

▽ *The lightness and equilibrated shape of the front and rear wings are emphasised by how perfectly they blend with the line of the flanks.*

Chassis and engine 2064 *(1954)*: John Simone, France
Chassis and engine 2065 *(1954)*: M. Roboly, France
Chassis and engine 2066 *(1954)*: Alberico Cacciari, Bologna
Chassis and engine 2067 *(1954)*: Bruno Venezian, Bologna
Chassis and engine 2068 *(1954)*: car for the Turin Motor Show
Chassis and engine 2069 *(1954)*: Sergio Ferraguti, Rome
Chassis and engine 2070 *(1954)*: Anna Maria Peduzzi, Como
Chassis and engine 2071 *(1954)*: J. Estager, France
Chassis and engine 2072 *(1954)*: John Simone, France,
for the 24 Hours of Le Mans
Chassis and engine 2073 *(1954)*: Argenzano
Chassis and engine 2074 *(1954)*: Luigi Bellucci, Naples
Chassis and engine 2075 *(1954)*: Bartolomeo Donato, Palermo
Chassis and engine 2076 *(1954)*: Alfonso De Portago, Spain
Chassis and engine 2077 *(1954)*: Siro Sbraci, Florence
Chassis and engine 2078 *(1954)*: Maserati works car
Chassis and engine 2079 *(1954)*: sports tourer for the Paris Motor Show
Chassis and engine 2080 *(1954)*: sold in the USA
Chassis and engine 2081 *(1954)*: sold in the USA
Chassis and engine 2082 *(1954)*: Maserati works car
Chassis and engine 2083 *(1955)*: Tom Friedman, USA
Chassis and engine 2084: Maria Teresa De Filippis, Naples
Chassis and engine 2085 *(1955)*: Gaetano Starabba, Palermo
Chassis and engine 2086 *(1955)*: Scuderia Centro-Sud, Rome
Chassis and engine 2087 *(1955)*: Attilio Buffa, Turin
Chassis and engine 2088 *(1955)*: Piero Valenzano, Turin
Chassis and engine 2089 *(1955)*: Francesco Giardini, Ferrara
Chassis and engine 2090 *(1955)*: Enzo and Ferdinando Lopez
Chassis and engine 2091 *(1955)*: Gigi Olivari, Cagliari
Chassis and engine 2092 *(1955)*: Bruno Sterzi, Milan
Chassis and engine 2093 *(1955)*: Candini-Landi
Engine 2095 *(1955)*: Brian Lister, Great Britain
Chassis and engine 2096 *(1955)*: Scuderia Centro-Sud, Rome
Chassis and engine 2097 *(1955)*: Luigi Bellucci, Naples
Chassis and engine 2098 *(1955)*: Maserati works car
Chassis and engine 2099 *(1955)*: Maserati works car

△ *The slender front wing is dominated by a large Marchal headlight.*

1955 Mille Miglia: Luigi Musso at the Ravenna control before his retirement.

▽ Francesco Giardini in his Maserati A6GCS during the 1955 Mille Miglia. He came fourth overall and won the 2000 Sport class at an average speed of 88.155 mph. (A. Sorlini – Giorgio Nada Editore Archives).

A6GCS
Pininfarina
berlinetta
(1953-1954)

A stylish masterpiece with a racing soul: the A6GCS Pininfarina berlinetta is one of the most fascinating Maseratis ever built and has a particularly interesting story to tell. The car was born on the initiative of Guglielmo Dei, Maserati's Roman concessionaire, with the intention of meeting the demands of some of his sporting customers, who wanted more racing comfort, particularly in bad weather. That is how the idea came about to build an A6GCS berlinetta, which became one of the few Maseratis to be bodied by Pininfarina and turned out to be the last of the Modena manufacturer's cars to be designed by the Turin artist. Just four examples of this berlinetta were built, one of which made the model's debut on the Pininfarina stand at the 1954 Turin Motor Show.

As far as the car's technical characteristics are concerned, the berlinetta was identical to the barchetta, with a six-cylinder 1985.6 cc engine, twin overhead camshafts, double ignition and a power output of 170 hp at 7300 rpm.

The berlinetta's chassis was the barchetta's tubular construction; front suspension was independent with upper and lower wishbones and helicoidal springs, the rear rigid live axle with semi-elliptic leaf springs and Houdaille dampers as well.

The difference between the two was to be found in the cars' starkly contrasting structures and, therefore, the weight of the two versions. The berlinetta was 40 mm lon-

continued on page 63

◁◁ *The arrow-shaped opening lever of the large petrol filler cap, high up on the rear pillar and made for rapid refuelling during a race.*

▽ *An aggressive yet harmonious line, a masterpiece in style that puts the Maserati berlinetta at the top of the list of the most attractively bodied cars built by Italian coachbuilders in the early Fifties.*

continued from page 60

ger than the barchetta (3880 mm against 3840 mm), 20 mm wider (1550 mm to 1530 mm), 290 mm higher (1150 mm against 860 mm). In addition, the berlinetta had a different interior and fuel tank capacity (125 litres to the barchetta's 115), and the berlinetta's weight was a mighty 260 kg more (1000 kg to 740 kg). Remarkably, the berlinetta's performance was not particularly penalised by such a large weight increase: maximum speed was almost identical at 143 mph to the barchetta's 146 mph, and acceleration times remained the same.

The first Pininfarina A6GCS was built in 1953 – the other three were all constructed in 1954 – and bought by Guglielmo Dei, before being sold to Count Gravina, a Sicilian nobleman who was a passionate racing motorist. That car, chassis number 2056, is the berlinetta illustrated here and one that boasts a very special story. In 1954, Gravina competed in the 14th Giro di Sicilia with his Pininfarina berlinetta, but was involved in a serious accident near Sciacca, in which his co-driver was killed.

With the front of the car destroyed and its chassis damaged, the sports tourer was sent back to Maserati at Modena, but the high cost of restoration induced Gravina to delay the work. That is why the berlinetta remained at Modena waiting to be repaired for three years. When work

continued on page 66

continued from page 63

did begin, Gravina decided to have his car re-bodied as a barchetta, but the cost of that was also considered too high, added to which the A6GCS was beginning to show its age on the technical and competitive fronts. From that moment, the situation became deadlocked: the cost of repairs continued to rise over the years, making the Count ever more hesitant about whether or not to proceed. In the end, an incredible 35 years slipped by but still the Pininfarina berlinetta languished in its dilapidated state. During that period, though, Maserati acquired the remains of the car and restoration work was carried out for the House of the Trident by Onofrio Campana in 1991.

Pininfarina bodied sports tourer chassis number 2057 was sold by Guglielmo Dei to Pietro Palmieri, a short man who had the height of the roof reduced by 4 cm compared to that of the other Pininfarina A6GCS berlinettas. However, excessive heat in the cockpit during the 1954 Giro dell'Umbria induced Palmieri to have the car re-bodied as a two-seater roadster. But the old bodyshell was kept intact by Giglielmo Dei and, in 1977, it was bought by an Italian collector: he had the Pininfarina body fitted to the chassis of A6GCS barchetta number 2070, which was powered by engine number 2080 from an identical car sold in the United States in 1954.

After having been on display at the 1954 Paris Motor Show in red with a broad white stripe stretching from nose to tail,

continued on page 68

△ A wrap-around windscreen between vertical pillars was of original design, inspired by those of numerous American cars of half a century ago.

▷△ The three-quarter rear view shows the harmonious flow between the flanks and the tail, dominated by a large, wrap-around rear window.

▷▽ The large, three-spoked wood-rimmed steering wheel in aluminium, which is almost vertical to the dashboard.

◁ The fuel tank's aluminium filler tube with rubber sleeve, seenthrough the rear window, emphasises the racing vocation of the car.

continued from page 66

sports tourer number 2059 was bought by Alberto Magi Diligenti, who had the car painted white before competing in the 1955 Mille Miglia with it under start number 643.

The fate of berlinetta chassis number 2060 is uncertain, although it is known it was later converted to a barchetta. The rarity of a Pininfarina-bodied Maserati, together with the few examples produced, has made this berlinetta one of the most significant models of all the cars produced by the House of the Trident, an outstanding example of equilibrium between racing engineering and refined elegance. And that is why this Pininfarina-bodied A6GCS won first prize in the GT class at the world-famous 2000 Concours d'Elegance at Pebble Beach, near Monterey, California. This important award at the American event, which takes place each year on the 18th fairway of the Pebble Beach Golf Club at the Pacific Ocean water's edge, was just tribute to one of the finest examples of Fifties Italian car design.

◁ The two chromed terminals of the exhaust system, set into the left hand side of the car, emphasise the sporting pedigree of the Pininfarina berlinetta. Immediately above is the logo of the legendary Turin coachbuilder.

▽ A subtle dome in Plexiglas protects the headlamps set into the wing, a feature dear to Pininfarina heart in the Fifties.

◁ To keep weight down, the cockpit of the car houses only the bare essentials. The large steering wheel and well-trimmed seats were developed to make the driver more comfortable when racing.

△ Simple, almost Spartan, the rear lights have chromed surrounds and directional indicators. Under the small circular cap is the engine oil filler cap.

▽ A tail of pure style and functional pragmatism. The absence of bumpers
confirms the strictly racing nature of the design project, while the suggestion of
fins on the rear wings that host the back lights dates the time of construction to
the early Fifties. The boot lid gives access to the spare wheel and nothing else.

Technical specifications

ENGINE

Front, longitudinal, six-cylinders in-line
Bore and stroke: 76.5x72 mm
Cubic capacity: 1985.6 cc
Valve gear: twin overhead camshafts, driven by gears
Number of valves: two per cylinder
Compression ratio: 9:1
Fuel feed: three Weber 40DCO3 carburettors
Ignition: double, with distributors
Cooling: water
Lubrication: dry sump
Maximum power: 170 hp at 7300 rpm

TRANSMISSION

Rear wheel drive
Clutch: dry multi-disc
Gearbox: four forward speeds plus reverse
Gear ratios: I) 0.452:1, II) 0.715:1; III) 0.847:1; IV) 1.1; R) 0.284:1
Axle ratio: 8/40

BODY

Two-seater berlinetta in aluminium

CHASSIS AND MECHANICS

Chassis: framework in elliptical-section tubes
Suspension: front – independent, upper and lower wishbones,
            coil springs, Houdaille hydraulic dampers;
            rear – rigid live axle, longitudinal semi-elliptic springs,
            Houdaille hydraulic dampers.
Brakes: hydraulically operated drums front and rear
Steering: worm and sector
Fuel tank: capacity 125 litres
Wheels: spoked, front 5.00x16, rear 6.00x16
Tyres: front 5.00x16, rear 6.00x16

DIMENSIONS AND WEIGHT

Wheelbase: 2310 mm
Track, front: 1335 mm
Track, rear: 1220 mm
Length: 3880 mm
Width: 1570 mm
Height: 1150 mm
Dry weight: 1000 kg

PERFORMANCE

Maximum speed: 143 mph

Chassis and engine numbers

Chassis and engine 2056 *(1953)*: Guglielmo Dei, Rome,
for Count Gravina
Chassis and engine 2057 *(1954)*: Guglielmo Dei, Rome,
for Pietro Palmieri
Chassis and engine 2059 *(1954)*: Exhibited at the Paris Motor Show
Chassis and engine 2060 *(1954)*: Guglielmo Dei, Rome

▷ *Pininfarina's signature on the
body of a Maserati is extremely
rare: but the celebrated Turin
designer placed his
unmistakable seal on this
magnificent berlinetta.*

▽ *The shiny battery of trumpets
belonging to the three Weber
40DCO3 carburettors add a
touch of elegance to the
narrow engine bay, and
perfectly proclaim the racing
vocation of the berlinetta.*

▷ *The two-tone Maserati A6GCS Pininfarina berlinetta made its debut in April 1954 at the Turin Motor Show. Just four of these cars were built.*

▽ *The 1955 Mille Miglia – the Pininfarina A6GCS number 643 (chassis number 2059) of A. Magi Diligenti and I. Minzoni, with its unusual white livery. (E. Ferraris - Giorgio Nada Editore Archives).*

250F
(1954-1958)

The most symbolic car in the history of Maserati is the 250F, to many one of the most beautiful single-seater racing cars ever built, and one that contributed decisively to increasing House of the Trident's prestige on the race tracks of the world. With Juan Manuel Fangio at the wheel of just such a car, Maserati won the 1957 Formula One World Championship, and so joined the exclusive club of manufacturers who have won the planet's maximum formula title. The sight of the Argentinean genius at the wheel of the sleek, long Italian racer became one of the most significant images in the history of the Maserati brand. But Fangio's 1957 single-seater was the final stage in an evolutionary project started four years earlier, based on a previous Formula 2 car and borrowing many of the A6GCM's components.

At first, the project was called the 250F1, in which the numbers stood for the maximum 2500 cc allowed by F1 rules for normally aspirated cars at the time. Later, it became known simply as the 250F, a name by which journalists the world over wrote and broadcast to hundreds of millions about the all-conquering Maserati.

The technical staff that created the successful single-seater was made up of Giulio Alfieri and Gioachino Colombo, who was involved in the initial phase of the project, Vittorio Bellentani and designer Nicola Di Mauro. Valerio Colotti worked on the development of the chassis and braking system, while Guerino Bertocchi took on the task of chief mechanic and test driver. The intention was to produce a car for sporting customers, to be sold at the relatively low price of Lit 6-7 million (about 13000 - 14000 US $). The first

continued on page 77

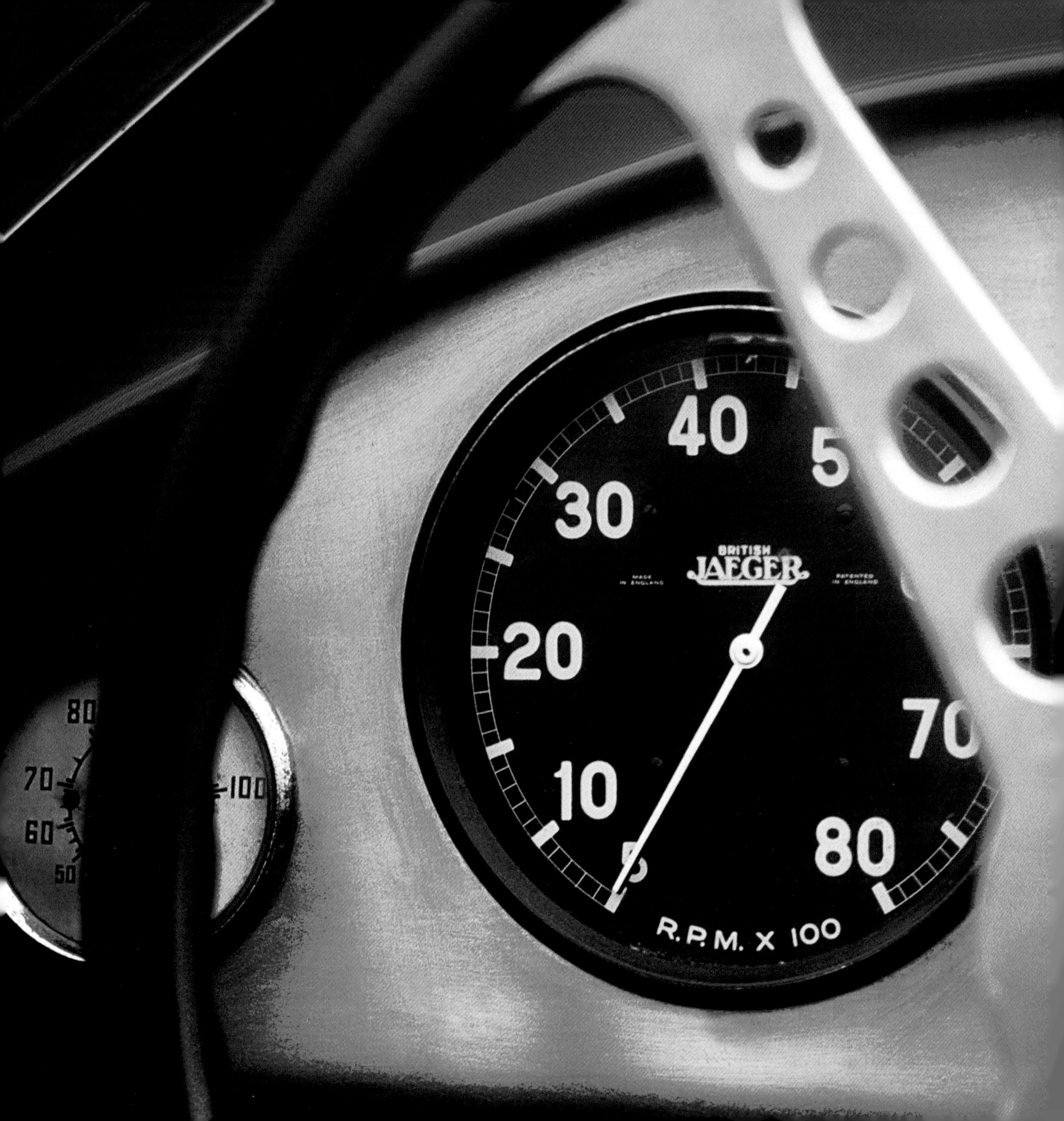
BRITISH
JAEGER
R.P.M. X 100

◁◁ *The black face of the big tachometer calibrated to 8000 rpm, with its large white needle and made by British Jaeger, stands out from the other instruments on the 250F's dashboard.*

△ *The paddle switch on the driver's right, used to regulate the two ignition magnetos.*

▽ *The twin overhead camshaft, six-cylinder in-line Maserati engine enlivened many a Formula One race between January 1954 and November 1957, the period in which the 2.5-litre formula was in force.*

continued from page 74

car was identified by the number of its chassis, 2501, and its notable performance characteristics attracted the attention of many professional drivers, among them Prince Birabongse Bhanudej Bhanubandh of Thailand, known as Bira in racing circles, who bought one of the first 250Fs – chassis number 2504 - and Roy Salvadori, who acquired 2507. Celebrated champions of the period including Stirling Moss, Juan Manuel Fangio and Jean Behra raced the 250F, constantly adding to its impressive list of successes. Technically, the new single-seater had a tubular chassis, characterised by its extremely rigid and complex structure. The engine took advantage of lessons learnt in the past and was a 2493.8 cc six-cylinder with double ignition and a bore and stroke of 84x75 mm, which produced 240 hp at

△ The imposing air intake on the right side of the bonnett dominates the 'shark's mouth' frontal area.

7200 rpm: a number of phases in its evolution continued to increase the car's power output until 1957, when it reached 270 hp at 8000 rpm. The two valves per cylinder were operated by twin overhead camshafts, driven by a gear cascade at the front of the engine. Lubrication was dry sump, while the fuel feed came from three Weber 42DCO3-45DCO3 carburettors, replaced in 1956 by an indirect injection system.

An early problem with the car was that the oil overheated in its reservoir, originally located to the right of the engine under the Weber carburettors. So the problem was solved by transferring the cell to the rear of the car, behind the fuel tank. The clutch housing protruded into the cockpit and was positioned almost between the driver's knees, while the pedal set-up had the clutch and accelerator on the left and the foot brake on the right. So the accelerator pedal was effectively in the centre, although the car driven by Stirling Moss, chassis number 2508, had the pedals in reverse order, as the British ace preferred his accelerator on the extreme right. The front suspension was of a system inspired by that of the Formula 2 single-seater, with two oscillating arms, helicoidal springs, hydraulic dampers and 14 mm stabiliser bar. But the rear suspension was a more innovative design, with a De Dion rear axle and transverse semi-elliptic upper springs, each composed of five leaves 4 or 3 mm thick. Various experimental modifications were carried out during the car's production cycle, and those that returned positive results were often carried forward to successive versions of the car. For example, the 250F that competed at Monza in 1956 had its engine at 6° to the car's longitudinal axis, so that the drive shaft could be placed to the left of the driving position to lower the Maserati's centre of gravity and improve aerodynamics. They were modifications that paid off, because Stirling Moss won that year's Grand Prix of Italy with chassis number 2525, set up in exactly that way: so the offset engine was retained for the remainder of the season.

Maserati also built an aerodynamic version of the 250F on chassis 2518: it had a much more streamlined body, with a full-width nose and tail sections and sleek pontoons between the front and rear wheels, but its career was short-lived. Jean Behra drove the car into fourth place in the 1955 Grand Prix of Italy at Monza and Harry Schell came fifth in it in the Syracuse GP, before the 250F streamliner

▽ Characteristic air vents open out on the much-rounded rear end to dispel air from the oil reservoir, slotted in behind the fuel tank.

continued on page 82

△ The shaped exhaust terminal is placed just above the height of the left rear wheel, close to the fuel tank.

▷ A detail of the independent front suspension. The picture shows the large winged brake drum.

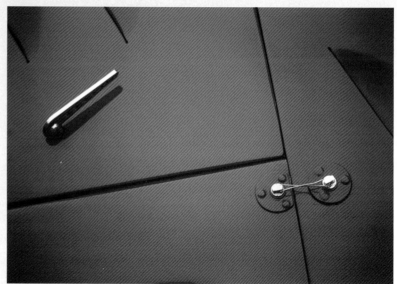

continued from page 78

was destroyed by fire at the Maserati factory. The 250F's long period of development drew to a close in 1957 with the re-design of the chassis, designated the T2, which was smaller, lighter and on which was built a new, lower aluminium body with a particularly refined, smooth line, completely different from the 1954 model. Known as the Lightweight, the first T2s were built on chassis numbers 2527, 2528 and 2529 and even today are considered the most beautiful single-seaters ever made.

The chassis was designed to host the new 12-cylinder V6 2490 cc engine, the development of which began in 1955. The bigger power plant produced 310 hp at 10,000 rpm and was designed to replace the venerable six-cylinder, which could be developed no further. After being installed as an experiment in chassis 2523, the new engine went through a demanding test programme before being entered for the 1957 Grand Prix of Italy, installed in T2 chassis number 2531 and driven by Jean Behra, who eventually retired with lubrication problems. Returning to 1954, the first 250Fs were, in reality, modified A6GCMs, with the 2.5 litre

△ *The Maserati 250F was given a new and lighter reticular-type chassis in small diameter tubing. The body took on a more streamlined and clear-cut appearance, and had spray guards behind the front wheels, which also revealed themselves to be extremely effective stabilisers.*

▷ *The aluminium petrol filler cap riveted to the fuel tank had a typical Maserati arrow-shaped tongue under the quick-release trigger, to speed up re-fuelling during rapid pit stops.*

△ With its exceptionally equilibrated shape, in its day, the 250F Lightweight was considered one of the most harmonious body designs in Formula 1.

◁ The spoked wheels of the
◁ 250F had a diameter of 16 inches, in some cases 17; tyres in sizes 6.50-7.00x16 or 7.00x17 were fitted to the rear wheels.

engine taking the place of the two-litre, the gearbox and engine fused together as one and a rigid rear live axle.

In the beginning, the car was designated as "provisional" by the factory and supplied to its "quicker" clients, while the 250F was honed to its definitive form. The first car, with its De Dion rear axle, all-in-one gearbox and differential, was number 2505 and which was completed in 1954 to become a works car driven by Juan Manuel Fangio, before it was sold in 1955 to French competitor André Simon.

The motor racing career of the 250F was both long and successful and spanned no less than seven years. Its first race was the Grand Prix of Argentina on 17 January 1954, won by Juan Manuel Fangio with 250F, and its last the 1960 United States Grand Prix at Riverside, making the 250F the only car to have competed in the first and last races of the 2.5-litre formula. During the Maserati's debut season, Fangio also won the Grand Prix of Belgium before returning to Mercedes-Benz, who had released him to drive for the House of the Trident until work on the development of their W196, with which he won the 1954 and 1955 Formula One World Championship, had been completed.

By the end of the 1954 season the 250F had scored a string of successes, including no less than 10 victories, in the hands of drivers like Prince Bira, Roy Salvadori and Stirling Moss. That year the great Englishman, four times runner-up in the F1 world championship, won the Aintree 200, the Gold Cup and Formula Libre races at Oulton Park, the Goodwood Trophy and Goodwood Cup and the Daily Telegraph Trophy at Aintree.

The 1955 season, dominated by Fangio and Moss in their Mercedes-Benz 196s, still saw the 250F win important races, including the Grand Prix of Pau, driven by Jean Behra, and the International Trophy race at Silverstone in the hands of 24-year-old Peter Collins. The retirement of Mercedes-Benz from motor racing, at the end of the 1955 season, more poured fuel on the fire of the eternal battle between Maserati and Ferrari the following year. In spite of his victories in the 1956 Grands Prix of Monaco and Italy, Stirling Moss was still unable to lay claim to the F1 world drivers' championship with his 250F, ending the season just three points away from Fangio, who took the title in his Lancia-Ferrari D50 with 30 points.

But for Maserati, 1957 became a year of retribution. The great Fangio won his record fifth world championship and his fourth consecutive title in the 250F having built up a huge points lead over Moss, who came second again, this time in a Vanwall. But in spite of winning the 1957 world championship, Maserati was unable to take commercial advantage of its great success. The company put together a programme to challenge for the 1958 title, but management problems and a major financial crisis led to the disbandment of the works F1 team.

At the end of 1958, which turned out to be as successful as it was dramatic, a new T3 chassis was under development for both six and 12-cylinder engines. Only two of the new chassis – 2533 and 2534 - were built in the "piccolo" or six-cylinder format. They were sold to Temple Buell's team in America and were driven by Masten Gregory and Carroll Shelby: 2534 was not only the last 250F but, sadly, the last single-seater produced by the Via Ciro Menotti factory.

△ The large steering wheel spokes in the small cockpit still allowed a clear view of the instruments.

▷▷ The Maserati 250F's cramped cockpit is dominated by the perforated, three-spoke steering wheel, the wrap-around seat designed to hold the driver firmly in fast corners and the long gear lever to the right of the seat.

▽ As well as aesthetics, the aerodynamic research carried out on the 250F "Lightweight" can also be seen in the rounded shape of the small windscreen.

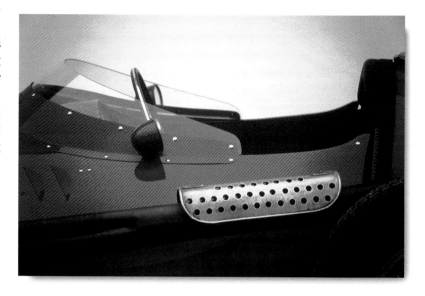

Technical specifications

ENGINE

Front, longitudinal, six cylinders in-line
Bore and stroke: 84x75
Cubic capacity: 2493.8 cc
Valve gear: twin overhead camshafts, gear driven
Number of valves: two per cylinder
Compression ratio: 12:1 (in 1958, 10.8:1)
Fuel feed: three Weber 42DCO3 - 45 DCO3 carburettors (from 1956, also
    indirect injection)
Ignition: double, with magnetos
Cooling: water
Lubrication: dry sump
Maximum power: 240/270 hp at 7200/8000 rpm

TRANSMISSION

Rear wheel drive
Clutch: dry multi-disc
Gearbox: four forward speeds plus reverse in a single unit
   with differential
Gear ratios: I) 0.466:1; II) 0.692:1; III) 0.833:1; IV) 1:1
Axle ratio: 45/15

BODY

Single-seater, in aluminium

CHASSIS AND MECHANICS

Chassis: tubular trellis (from 1957 reticular)
Suspension: front – independent, upper and lower
    wishbones, coil springs, Houdaille hydraulic dampers;
    rear – De Dion axle, transverse semi-elliptic
    leaf spring, Houdaille hydraulic dampers
Brakes: hydraulically operated drums front and rear
Steering: worm and sector
Fuel tank: capacity 200 litres
Wheels: spoked, front 5.50x16, rear 5.50x16 – 7.00x16
Tyres: front 5.25x16 – 5.50x16 – 6.50x16; rear 6.50x16 – 7.00x16 –
  7.00x17

DIMENSIONS AND WEIGHT

Wheelbase: 2280 mm (2225 mm in 1957 and 2200 mm in 1958)
Track, front: 1300 mm (1310 mm in 1958)
Track, rear: 1250 mm
Length: 4050 mm
Width: 980 mm
Height: 950 mm
Weight: 630/670 kg (550 kg in 1958)

PERFORMANCE

Maximum speed: 180 mph

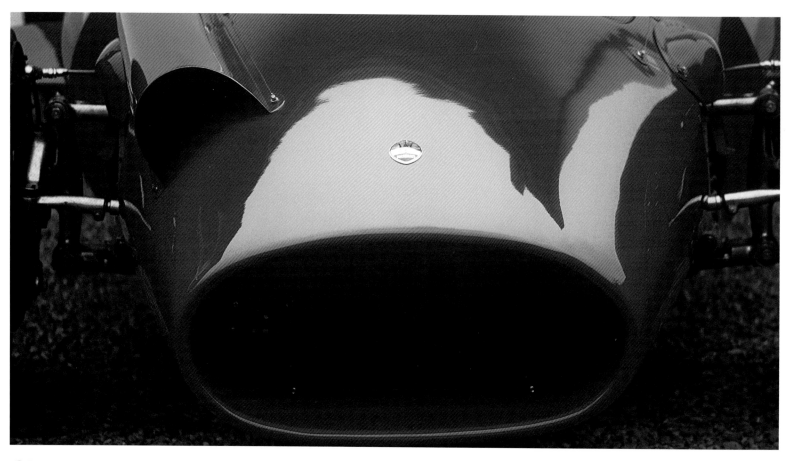

Chassis and engine numbers

Chassis and engine 2501 *(1954):* works car exhibited at the Paris Motor Show

Chassis and engine 2502 *(1954):* ex-A6GCM, Jorge Da Ponte, Argentina

Chassis and engine 2503 *(1954):* ex-A6GCM for Harry Schell, France

Chassis and engine 2504 *(1954):* ex-A6GCM for Prince Bira, Thailand

Chassis and engine 2505 *(1954):* Maserati works car

Chassis and engine 2506 *(1954):* Maserati works car for Onofre Marimon

Chassis and engine 2507 *(1954):* Gilby Engineering, London, for Roy Salvadori

Chassis and engine 2508 *(1954):* Maserati works car for Stirling Moss

△ *A metal grill to protect the radiator covered the elliptical air intake, in which the starting handle aperture is housed. On the car's right is the long air intake that feeds into the Weber carburettors.*

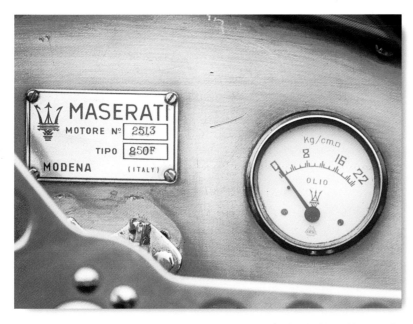

△ On the dashboard is a small
Maserati identification plaque,
bearing the engine number
and describing the type of
car.

▽ The front profile, with its air intake.

Chassis and engine 2509 *(1954):* Owen Organisation, Great Britain

Chassis and engine 2510 *(1954):* ex-A6GCM for Emanuel De Graffenried, Switzerland

Chassis and engine 2511 *(1954):* Maserati works car for Sergio Mantovani

Chassis and engine 2512 *(1954):* Maserati works car for Onofre Marimon

Chassis 2513 *(1954):* chassis only for Tony Vandervell, Great Britain

Chassis and engine 2514 *(1954):* Maserati works car for Luigi Musso and Sergio Mantovani

Chassis and engine 2515 *(1955):* Maserati works car for Roberto Mieres and Carroll Shelby

Chassis and engine 2516 *(1955):* Maserati works car for Jean Behra

Chassis and engine 2518 *(1955):* Maserati works car with aerodynamic body

Chassis and engine 2519 *(1956):* Luigi Piotti, Italy

Chassis and engine 2520 *(1956):* Maserati works car for José Froilan Gonzales

Chassis and engine 2521 *(1956):* Maserati works car

Chassis and engine 2522 *(1956):* Maserati works car

Chassis and engine 2523 *(1956):* Maserati works car

Chassis and engine 2524 *(1956):* Francisco Godia-Sales, Spain

Chassis and engine 2525 *(1956):* Maserati works car for Stirling Moss

Chassis and engine 2526 *(1956):* Maserati works car for Jean Behra

Chassis 2527, engine 2526 *(1956)* Maserati works car for Juan Manuel Fangio and Harry Schell

Chassis and engine 2528 *(1956):* Maserati works car for Juan Manuel Fangio and Harry Schell

Chassis and engine 2529 *(1956):* Maserati works car for Juan Manuel Fangio and Harry Schell

Chassis and engine 2530 *(1957):* Maserati T2 works car with 12-cylinder engine

Chassis and engine 2531 *(1957):* Maserati T2 works car with 12-cylinder engine for Jean Behra

Chassis and engine 2532 *(1958):* Maserati T3 works car

Chassis and engine 2533 *(1958):* T3 for the Temple Buell Team, USA.

Chassis and engine 2534 *(1958):* T3 for the Temple Buell Team, USA

△ 2 February 1958, Grand Prix of Argentina: Juan Manuel Fangio slicing through track surface water as he drives T2 chassis number 2529, one of the last of the 250Fs, to victory after Maserati had officially retired from Formula One motor racing.

△ 2 October 1954: Stirling Moss winning the Daily Telegraph Trophy race at Aintree in the mechanical fuel injection 250F, chassis number 2508.

▷ A Maserati 250F T2 V12 being tested in 1957 by Jean Behra.

150S
(1955-1957)

"This car doesn't hold the road". Having just climbed out of a rigid rear axle A6GCS, that was often the comment of some drivers after trying the new, more modern 150S with its equally new De Dion rear axle; but they were wrong. Maserati's new sports car soon had its chance to prove them so in the hands of Jean Behra, who won the 500 kms of the Nürburgring with 150S chassis number 1656 on 28 August 1955. The car made no bones about forcefully distinguishing itself on the legendary German circuit, even though it was up against some tough competition, including no less than 13 Porsches and four EMW. The origin of the 150S project harks back to 1953, when the House of the Trident decided to look beyond the borders of its homeland and open up new markets. It's name had become popular among many American servicemen, many of them still stationed in Italy, through the exploits of its earlier cars and drivers, among them the tremendous achievement of Wilbur Shaw in winning the legendary Indianapolis 500 in a Maserati 8CTF not once, which would have been a giant killer of a result anyway, but an astounding twice, in 1939 and 1940. On top of which the victorious Maserati 250F continued that tradition as a leading contender for the period's Formula One honours on the racing circuits of the world.

A reduced cubic capacity was selected for the 150S because of the preference shown by potential clients for the 1500 sport category, until that time dominated by British and German cars. But Maserati's extensive involvement in many other areas of motor racing was delaying the development of the new sports car: so to make up for lost time, a supplementary test programme was drawn up in October 1954, in which the new four-cylinder in-line 1484.1 cc engine with twin overhead camshafts and double ignition was installed in the Maria Luisa IV racing speedboat of Liborio

continued on page 95

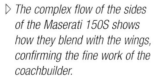

◁ *With the exception of the tachometer, the instrument dials of the 150S had an original two-tone colour.*

continued from page 92

Guidotti, who dominated his sport in the Fifties. Later, the engine was fitted to a 150S with a considerable reduction in its compression ratio, down from the 11.5:1 of the racing speedboat, which was fuelled by an alcohol mixture, to the 9:1 of the road-going engine. The project manager was Vittorio Bellentani, but the car was also developed with feedback from Guerino Bertocchi, the legendary Maserati chief mechanic and test driver, who had organised an important test session in April 1955, involving a number of clients. The road qualities of the 150S that emerged from that test driving steered the car in the direction of highly expert racing driver customers. But a long gestation period meant the definitive version of the new Maserati did not make its debut until 1955, after a decision had been taken on its type of chassis and suspension. The choice came down on the side of the most innovative alternative, compared to ideas contemplated at the start of the project, which would have led to a hybrid car with many of its components coming from the A6GCS, such as the rigid rear axle and independently suspended front wheels. The development team took a more innovative approach so that the first 150S, chassis number 1652, was the result of an advanced engineering project for its era.

The new car was given a De Dion rear axle, new front suspension, a new type of gearbox, with four forward gears and Porsche synchromesh, plus a single fusion engine and gearbox. After 1956, the car was fitted with a five-speed 'box and a self-locking ZF differential.

▷ *The complex flow of the sides of the Maserati 150S shows how they blend with the wings, confirming the fine work of the coachbuilder.*

The responsibility for designing and building the body was given to Celestino Fiandri and turned out rather similar to the 300S but, obviously, in smaller scale. The wheelbase of the second 150S, chassis number 1653, was lengthened by 1000 mm.

Having seen the improvements made to the 150S as a result of customer testing, the project team decided to put all those modifications into production from chassis number 1656. From 1956, coach building was switched to Medardo Fantuzzi, who "dressed" the 150S in more streamlined and aerodynamic "clothes" from chassis numbers 1665, 1666 and 1667.

The racing career of the 150S culminated in 1956 with its victory in the Five Hours of Messina, driven by Amelio Garavaglia, and ninth overall in the 24 Hours of Le Mans, crewed by Claude Bourillot and Henri Perroud. But Maserati's excessive diversification and the large number of models it produced stopped the company from further developing the car so that its competitiveness could be

continued on page 100

▷ *The pictures on this page show the attention paid to the 150S body's aerodynamics; for example, the oil reservoir cap was set into the rear bodywork. The shape of the numerous air intakes was flush and carefully designed to relay the maximum amount of fresh air to the engine bay and ensure the effective evacuation of hot air.*

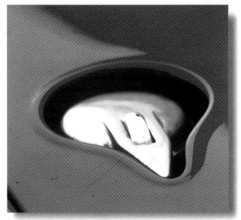

△ The similarity can easily be seen between the four-cylinder 150S and the
bigger, more powerful six-cylinder 300S. The most obvious difference is in the
front end of the two cars, shorter and more rounded for the 1500 cc sports
car and a long nose for the 300S. The 1500 cc does not have the
aerodynamic headrest that appeared behind the driver on some 300S models.
The harmonious flow of the sides, similar on both cars, accommodated a large
grill behind the front wheels for the ejection of hot air from the engine
compartment.

continued from page 96

maintained, and it was decided to discontinue production of the car at the end of 1956. But after further development, its 1484 cc engine lived on: at the request of a number of clients, it was supplied for installation in the ultra-modern rear-engined Formula Two cars that began to emerge in the Sixties, with chassis designed in Great Britain.

A change in motor sport rules enabled Scuderia Centro-Sud to build a Formula One Cooper-Maserati with the engine, which was entered for the Grand Prix of Pau, France and driven by the American, Masten Gregory.

After its various stages of evolution, the Maserati 1500 cc engine eventually developed a power output of 165 hp at 8500 rpm and was given various components in aluminium and magnesium alloy, which reduced its weight to "only" 130 kg. In that final configuration, the engine was called the T6 and was sold to private entrants for around Lit 2.5 million (about 4000 US $).

▷ *The front light grouping was covered with Plexiglas, rounded to the curve of the wing to optimise aerodynamic efficiency and improve the car's aesthetic appeal. Spoked wheels with central wing nuts reveal the large-diameter drum brakes.*

▽ *The run of the exhaust pipes along the lower left flank of the 150S was typical of Maserati sports car design and similar to the A6GCS. Aluminium filler caps can be seen on the rear bodywork of the car, the larger for fuel and the smaller for engine oil.*

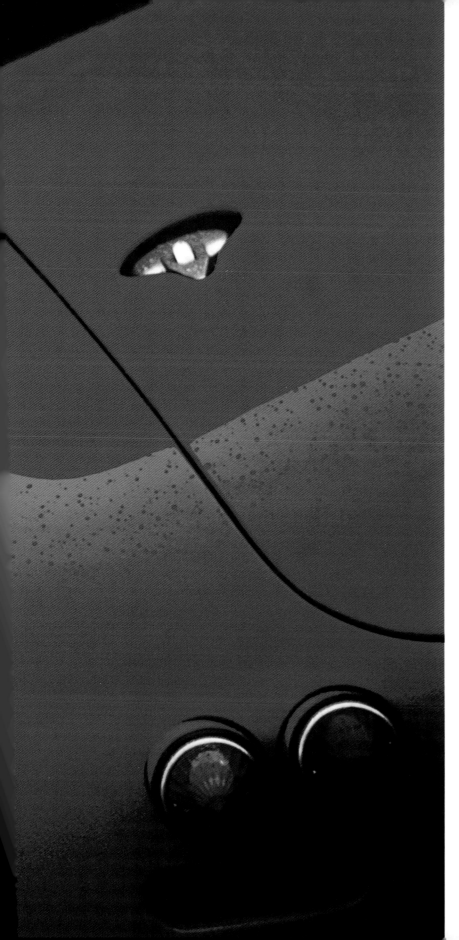

Technical specifications

ENGINE

Front, longitudinal, four cylinders in-line
Bore and stroke: 81x72 mm
Cubic capacity: 1484.1 cc
Valve gear: twin overhead camshafts driven by gears
Number of valves: two per cylinder
Compression ratio: 9:1
Fuel feed: two Weber 45DCO3 carburettors
Ignition: double, with distributors or magnetos
Cooling: water
Lubrication: dry sump
Maximum power: 140 hp at 7500 rpm

TRANSMISSION

Rear wheel drive
Clutch: dry multi-disc
Gearbox: four forward speeds plus reverse (from 1956 also five-speed)
Gear ratios: I) 1.895:1; II) 1.525:1; III) 1.110:1; IV) 1:1; R) 2.22:1
Axle ratio: 9/40

BODY

Two-seater roadster, in aluminium

CHASSIS AND MECHANICS

Chassis: tubular trellis structure
Suspension: front – independent, upper and lower wishbones, coil
springs, Houdaille hydraulic dampers; rear
De Dion axle, transverse semi-elliptic leaf spring, Houdaille
hydraulic dampers
Brakes: hydraulically operated drums front and rear
Steering: worm and sector
Fuel tank: capacity 125 litres
Wheels: spoked, 4.50x16
Tyres: front 5.12x16; rear 5.50x16

DIMENSIONS AND WEIGHT

Wheelbase: 2150 mm (2250 mm)
Track, front: 1250 mm
Track, rear: 1200 mm
Length: 3800 mm
Width: 1500 mm
Height: 980 mm
Dry weight: 630 kg

PERFORMANCE

Maximum speed: 143 mph

Chassis and engine numbers

Engine 1650 *(1955):* racing speedboat Maria Luisa IV
Chassis and engine 1651 *(1955):* prototype
Chassis and engine 1652 *(1955):* Leopardi, Rome
Chassis and engine 1653 *(1955):* Isabelle Haskell, USA
Chassis and engine 1654 *(1955):* Tephenier, Paris
Chassis and engine 1655 *(1955):* Tony Parravano, USA
Chassis and engine 1656 *(1955):* Maserati works car
Chassis and engine 1657 *(1955):* Briggs Cunningham, USA
Engine 1658 *(1955):* Tephenier, Paris, for chassis number 1654
Chassis and engine 1659 *(1955):* sold in the USA
Chassis and engine 1660 *(1956):* Alejandro De Tomaso, Argentina
Chassis and engine 1661 *(1956):* exhibited at the Geneva Motor Show
Chassis and engine 1662 *(1956):* owner unknown
Chassis and engine 1663 *(1956):* owner unknown
Chassis and engine 1664 *(1956):* owner unknown
Chassis and engine 1665 *(1956):* owner unknown
Chassis and engine 1666 *(1956):* Brian Naylor, Great Britain
Chassis and engine 1667 *(1956):* Maserati works car
Chassis and engine 1668 *(1956):* owner unknown
Chassis and engine 1669 *(1956):* owner unknown
Chassis and engine 1670 *(1956):* owner unknown
Chassis and engine 1671 *(1956):* Maserati works car
Chassis and engine 1672 *(1956):* Maserati works car
Chassis and engine 1673 *(1956):* owner unknown
Chassis and engine 1674 *(1956):* Maserati works car
Chassis and engine 1675 *(1957):* owner unknown
Engine 1676 *(1957):* Brian Naylor, Great Britain
Engine ? *(1957):* Fantuzzi bodied cabriolet
Engine 4 *(1955):* for boat use

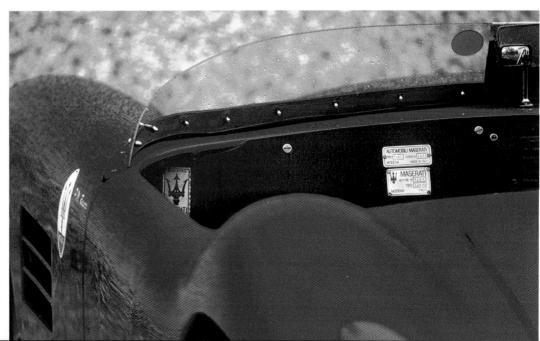

▷ 28 August 1955, Nürburgring 500 Kilometres: Jean Behra driving 150S chassis number 1656 to the model's first international race victory. The new Maserati sports car beat combat-hardened opposition to the chequered flag, including 13 Porsches and four EMWs, which augmented the intrinsic value of the car's win.

200S/SI
(1955-1957)

The new Maserati 200S sports car had a tough battle on its hands, trying to match the success of its glorious elder sister, the A6GCS. But when it did go racing in 1955 for the House of the Trident, it won and later became a commercial success, too. The development project that Via Ciro Minotti came up with for the car that was to stand toe-to-toe with the Ferrari 500 Mondial got off the ground in 1953: it was based on the 4CF2 engine of a year earlier which, in its sports car guise, was designated the Type 52. To speed up work on the new car and cut costs, the development of the 200S and the smaller 150S went ahead in tandem. The bigger car's engine was a four-cylinder in-line with twin overhead camshafts, two valves per cylinder and double ignition through two magnetos, later substituted by the same number of coils; with a rather high compression ratio of 9.8:1, the power unit returned 190 hp at 7500 rpm. The high power output of the new engine and, in particular, the car's power curve suggested the adoption of a ZF self-locking differential and, on many examples, the use of a five-speed synchromesh gearbox as an alternative to the traditional four-speed.

The 200S chassis, which was identical to the ovoid and round tubed structure of the 150S, had a live rear axle derived from that of the A6GCS, instead of the more modern and sophisticated De Dion of its smaller sister car. But after the production of several examples of the 200S with the older technology axle (chassis numbers 2401, 2402 and 2405) and following a number of client requests, development testing induced the project team to consider adopting the De Dion rear axle for production cars, a component

continued on page 111

◁ *The 200SI's harmony of shape and a number of design details embody a style that was well consolidated by the Italian school of coachbuilders.*

continued from page 108

already fitted to the 150S. The evolution of the 200S in the second phase of its development after chassis 2405 resulted in the use of a trellis-type chassis, made by Gilco and modified by Maserati. In that period, the aluminium design was also changed: after Celestino Fiandri, who built bodies for the first five cars, the chassis from number 2405 were switched to Medardo Fantuzzi, who built all subsequent examples. This aesthetic evolution transformed the shape of the first few cars, which were rounder and more solid, into Fantuzzi's sleek, elegant 200S lines.

The sales success of the car is a testimonial to the notable number of cars produced – 28 between 1955 and 1957, plus five engines. In 1957 the car was modified to conform to new Sport category regulations and its designation was changed to 200SI or Sport International.

The SI adopted a number of features that were, perhaps, little in keeping with a thoroughbred sports car, including a thin canvas top for the protection, more imaginary than real, of the driver, as well as wipers for the larger surface windscreen; the doors were also of reduced dimensions.

The aesthetic result of these modifications was somewhat dubious and robbed the 200SI of some of the fascination that emanated from its first 200S incarnation.

continued on page 114

▷ *The gear lever and handbrake were incorporated in the aluminium transmission bell housing.*

continued from page 111

The sports career of the 200S and 200SI included a number of important successes, culminating in winning the 1957 European Hillclimb Championship in the hands of Switzerland's Willy Daetwyler.

Other significant race results included second in the Supercortemaggiore Grand Prix, driven by Stirling Moss and Cesare Perdisa, on 24 June 1956, after an extremely unlucky race in which the Maserati was roundly beaten by the new Ferrari Testarossa.

The dynamic qualities of the 200S and its new De Dion rear axle came to the fore at the next Grand Prix of Bari on 22 July, which was won by Jean Behra: the Frenchman also came first in the Grand Prix of Rome on 21 October.

Giorgio Scarlatti's third place in the Giro di Sicilia on 14 April 1957 was one of the last successes of this Maserati model and an event in which the car's excellent handling qualities were there for all to see.

This was mainly due to the De Dion rear axle, which performed well in the hands of professional drivers but put gentlemen drivers, the principal buyers of the 200S/SI, in difficulty as they could not fully exploit the car.

But the reason for the decline of this model can more easily be found in the severe management crisis that was slowly suffocating Maserati, as well as the wide-range of motor sport activities in which the company was so extensively involved.

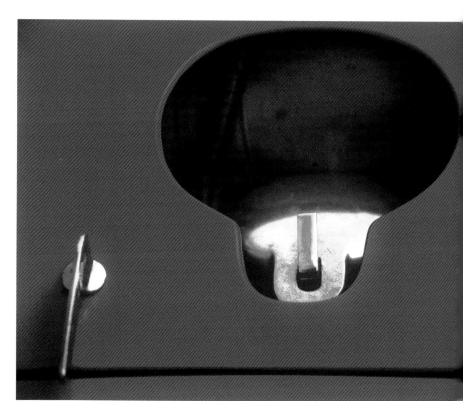

△ *The quick-release aluminium filler cap for fast refuelling is almost hidden in its housing, set deep into the boot lid.*

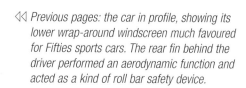

◁◁ *Previous pages: the car in profile, showing its lower wrap-around windscreen much favoured for Fifties sports cars. The rear fin behind the driver performed an aerodynamic function and acted as a kind of roll bar safety device.*

◁ *The three air vents on the sides expel hot air from the engine bay and front brakes.*

△ The Maserati 200SI chassis number 2406
photographed for this chapter left the
factory on 17 August 1956. Its sleek body
is the work of Medardo Fantuzzi, one of
the Trident's trusted coachbuilders. Like
most Maserati sports racers of the Fifties,
each car had the strong personality of the
period's most prestigious thoroughbreds.

◁◁ The front end view shows the large trident mounted inside the yawning front air intake. The detail is among the classic features of Fifties Maseratis, making them immediately recognisable. Note the elegant blending of the two wings with the bonnet.

▷ Set into a brushed aluminium dashboard are Jaeger's circular instruments, the biggest diameter dial being the tachometer. On the left are the water temperature and oil pressure gauges. The position of the rev counter's calibration is different to today's, with the 0 marker top right and the maximum 10,000 rpm revs top left.

△ An essential cockpit, in accordance with the best racing car traditions. Prominent features include the hinged pedal lay-out, large diameter wood-rimmed steering wheel, bare instruments and the close-gate gear lever.

Technical specifications

ENGINE

Front, longitudinal, four cylinders in line
Bore and stroke: 92x75 mm
Cubic capacity: 1994.3 cc
Valve gear: twin overhead camshafts driven by gears
Number of valves: two per cylinder
Compression ratio: 9,8:1 (9.5:1)
Fuel feed: two Weber 45DCO3 carburettors
Ignition: double, with distributors or magnetos
Cooling: water
Lubrication: dry sump
Maximum power: 186 hp at 7500 rpm (190 hp at 7800 rpm)

TRANSMISSION

Rear wheel drive
Clutch: dry multi-disc
Gearbox. Four or five forward speeds plus reverse
Gear ratios: I) 15.29:1; II) 17.21:1; III) 19.19:1; IV) 21.17:1; R) 2.22:1
Axle ratio: 9/40

BODY

Two-seater roadster, in aluminium

CHASSIS AND MECHANICS

Chassis: tubular, trellis structure
Suspension: front – independent, upper and lower wishbones, coil
springs and Houdaille hydraulic dampers; rear De Dion–
axle, transverse leaf spring and Houdaille hydraulic
dampers
Brakes: hydraulically operated drums front and rear
Steering: worm and sector
Fuel tank: capacity 120 litres (130 litres)
Wheels: spoked, 5.00x16 (4.50x16)
Tyres: front 5.50x16 – 6.00x16; rear 5.50x16 – 6.00x16 (front 5.50x16;
rear 6.50x16)

DIMENSIONS AND WEIGHT

Wheelbase: 2150-2250 mm (2150 mm)
Track, front: 1250 mm
Track, rear: 1200 mm
Length: 3900 mm
Width: 1450 mm
Height: 980 mm
Dry weight: 670 kg (660 kg)

PERFORMANCE

Maximum speed: 155 mph (162 mph)

(NB: 200SI figures are in brackets).

△ Part of the trellis structure tubular chassis is concealed within the car's aluminium body, the proportions of which respect the aesthetic trends of Fifties sports cars. The exhaust, set into its own housing along the side of the car, harks back to celebrated Maseratis like the 1953 A6GCS. The spoked wheels, held in place by winged wheel nuts, are size 6.00x16.

▷▷ Maserati's oval trident badge is the only embellishment permitted on the front of the car.

▷▷ The aerodynamic faring behind the driving position is held in place by a chrome catch.

▷▷ The classic Maserati bonnet lever, perforated for lightness.

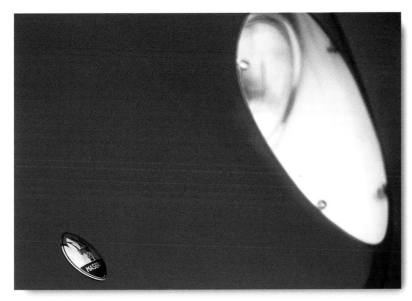

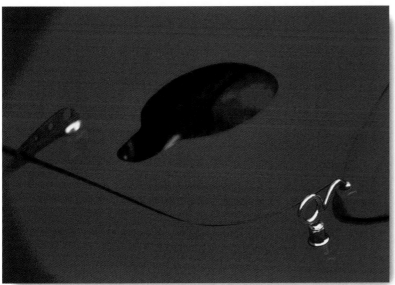

Chassis and engine numbers

Chassis and engine 2401 *(1955):* Maserati works car
Chassis and engine 2402 *(1956):* Gilberto Cornacchia, Milan
Chassis and engine 2403 *(1956):* Maserati works car
Chassis and engine 2404 *(1956):* Maserati works car
Chassis and engine 2405 *(1956):* Maserati works car
Chassis and engine 2406 *(1956):* owner unknown
Chassis and engine 2407 *(1956):* ex-150S number 1672
Chassis and engine 2408 *(1956):* owner unknown
Chassis and engine 2409 *(1957):* Mennato Boffa, Naples
Chassis and engine 2412 *(1957):* owner unknown
Chassis and engine 2413 *(1957):* owner unknown
Chassis and engine 2414 *(1957):* owner unknown
Chassis and engine 2415 *(1957):* owner unknown
Chassis and engine 2416 *(1957):* owner unknown
Chassis and engine 2417 *(1957):* Bruno Ruffo, Verona
Chassis and engine 2418 *(1957):* owner unknown
Chassis and engine 2419 *(1957):* Piero Giannotti, Viareggio
Chassis and engine 2420 *(1957):* owner unknown
Chassis and engine 2421 *(1957):* owner unknown
Chassis and engine 2422 *(1957):* owner unknown
Chassis and engine 2423 *(1957):* owner unknown
Chassis and engine 2424 *(1957):* owner unknown
Chassis and engine 2425 *(1957):* owner unknown
Chassis and engine 2426 *(1957):* owner unknown
Chassis and engine 2427 *(1957):* owner unknown
Chassis and engine 2428 *(1957):* owner unknown
Chassis and engine 2429 *(1957):* owner unknown
Chassis and engine 2430 *(1957):* Alan Connel, USA

▽ *16 August 1957: Willy Daetwyler winning*
the Salzburg, Austria, round of the
European Hillclimb Championship in a
Maserati 200SI.

▽ *Franco Bordoni in a Maserati 200SI at the start of the 1957 Mille Miglia. The car was one of the most competitive in the up to 2000 cc sport class, but was forced to retire after 6h 32' 24" (A. Sorlini - Giorgio Nada Editore Archives).*

300S
(1955-1958)

The 300s' victory in the 1000 Kilometres of the Nürburgring in the hands of Stirling Moss and Jean Behra on 27 May 1956, is still remembered today as one of Maserati's greatest successes: a race won the hard way, against tough opposition. From the outset, the British ace forced his opponents and their Ferraris, Aston Martins and Jaguars to maintain an extremely fast pace if they were to stay in the hunt. The British cars soon began to lose ground and the opposition eventually boiled down to Juan Manuel Fangio and Eugenio Castellotti in a Ferrari 860 Monza, which was even able to take the lead at one stage in the German marathon. But an unscheduled pit stop by the Ferrari to take on more fuel let Moss back into the lead and he won at an average speed of 80.61 mph.

In spite of this and the Maserati's success in other races, among them the 1000 Kilometres of Buenos Aires, the 1956 World Sports Car Championship still went to Ferrari, although Moss topped the drivers' table, equal first with Ferrari's Eugenio Castellotti.

Instituted in 1953, the World Sports Car Championship became so popular it even began to rival Formula One in enthusiasts' affections.

Stirling Moss' success in 1956 was just reward for a notable technical effort by Maserati, which had no great experience in big-engined sport car racing: instead, for three years it had campaigned the A6GCS, which was a point of reference in two-litre competition. The three-litres and more that dominated the new world championship, an area in which the most illustrious names in European motor racing put themselves to the test, was a completely new ball game

continued on page 129

△ The 300S retains the hallmarks of previous Maserati sports models: cramped cockpit, basic instruments, large diameter steering wheel, easily accessible controls; all in line with the best racing traditions of the day.

▽ The driving position of the 300S is almost a replica of that of the Monofaro. On the extreme left of the dashboard there is the tachometer marked up to a maximum of 10,000 rpm, on the right a switch for the regulation of the ignition magnetos.

continued from page 126

to the House of the Trident. The origins of the 300S go back to 1954, when a prototype called the 250S was built: the car was powered by an engine derived from the 250F Grand Prix car and had a cubic capacity of 2500 cc; but it was penalised by running on petrol instead of a mixture of alcohol used at the time in Formula One, and was only able to drum up 230 hp at 7000 rpm with its 9:1 compression ratio.

Lowered into an A6GCS chassis and hooked up to a four-speed gearbox, the engine participated unsuccessfully in the 1954 Mille Miglia; driven by Mantovani and Palazzi, the car retired before the Ravenna control. But that failure did not discourage Maserati, who built a new right-hand drive prototype to compete in the Supercortemaggiore Grand Prix at Monza, driven by Juan Manuel Fangio and Onofre Marimon: the 250S did well, but eventually had to retire with a broken De Dion rear axle.

The Maserati technical staff, headed by Vittorio Bellentani, analysed the race and highlighted the 250S' substantial lack of power against that of its bigger-engined opponents. Bellentani and his team came to the conclusion that they had to modify their project by bringing in a new 2800 cc engine, which was immediately rejected after being tested by Guerino Bertocchi and Luigi Villoresi. So it was decided to develop a new six cylinder in-line 2992.5 cc power unit, derived directly from the 250F, but with a much lower compression ratio of 9:1 instead of the Grand Prix car's 12:1. The new sports car engine developed 245 hp at 6200 rpm, a relatively composed and safe revolution ratio compared to the single-seater which, in its first configuration, put out 240 hp at 7200 rpm: the 300S power plant produced almost the same amount of power, but without punishing its mechanics and by using a traditional cylinder head with twin overhead camshafts and double ignition.

Its chassis was carefully developed and comprised a trellis of elliptical and round-section tubing, a transverse gearbox, which was all in one with the differential, and a De Dion rear axle. First, the chassis was built in-house by Maserati: it was not until later that its construction was entrusted to Gilco of Milan.

continued on page 132

continued from page 129

Medardo Fantuzzi built the body, inspired by the coach buil-ding trends of the period's sports cars. In accordance with sports car category rules, the driving position was protec-ted by a reduced height windscreen that was very much of the wrap-around type and linked up with the rear headrest. Among the most distinctive characteristics that immediately singled out the 300S were the generous air outlets along the sides behind the front wings and the shaping of the rear end, in which the oil (20 kg) and fuel (150 litres) tanks were housed. In compliance with the regulations of the day, the car had two miniscule doors so that the driver could board the car more easily, but they were so small they were inef-fectual.

The 1955 motor racing season was not kind to the 300S, which had a new car's usual share of teething troubles, after its positive debut (third and fourth overall) in the 12 Hours of Sebring. The car's Mille Miglia outing in May trans-formed itself into a disaster, with Cesare Perdisa threathe-ning Fangio's second place before being forced to retire. A few days later, Luigi Musso came third with the 300S in the Giro di Sicilia, while at the 24 Hours of Le Mans in June the Luigi Musso and Piero Valenzano car retired during the 19th hour and the Roberto Mieres-Cesare Perdisa 300S went out five hours after the start. One of the year's bright spots was when Juan Manuel Fangio won the Grand Prix of Venezuela, the last major race of the year, in the Maserati 300S. But the fact was that in most of its 1955 races, one

continued on page 135

▷ The rear end of the 300S is dominated by the ample flow of the wings and the limited overhang of the tail.

◁ The aerodynamic fairing of the headrest is fixed to the boot lid with much riveting, as was the trend with the aluminium bodies of the Fifties.

◁ *The disposition of the air vents is evidence of the careful studies made by the designers of the period of how best to extract heat from the engine compartment.*

▽ *The extraordinary balance of shape that Medardo Fantuzzi was able to bring to the 300S is still today an outstanding example of stylish car design of the period.*

△ The two vertical air intakes on the car's back end dissipated hot air from the rear axle.

▽ Extremely elegant and in line with the classic dictates of the Trident, the stylish design of the frontal area, with its smooth surfaces shaped with mastery, especially the area in which the wings blend with the bonnet.

continued from page 132

major problem that dogged the three-litre Mascrati: lack of power. The following year went better for the sleek 300S. It started with Stirling Moss and Carlos Menditeguy winning the 1000 Kms of Argentina in the car on 29 January; Behra came third in it at the Grand Prix of Dakar and Piero Taruffi second in the 1956 Giro di Sicilia. But Taruffi was forced to retire from the year's Mille Miglia due to the poor preparation by the company of his and the other 30 Maseratis entered for the legendary Brescian race.

Then came the Moss-Behra victory in the Nürburgring 1000 Kms, Taruffi's second place in the Targa Florio, the Behra-Louis Rosier win in the Montlhéry 1000 Kms, the Moss-Perdisa second place in the Supercortemaggiore Grand Prix at Monza and the spectacular success in the Grand Prix of Bari, where Moss came first, Taruffi fourth and Benoit Musy fifth, all in Maserati 300Ss.

A number of important modifications were carried out to the car during the course of its racing career. From chassis number 3063 in 1956, the front end was lengthened to better the 300s' aerodynamics.

The engine's fuel system was improved by a number of changes derived from the evolution of the 250F's power plant, including the adoption of Weber 45DCO3 carburettors from chassis 3057 onwards, and the subsequent fruitless experiments with direct fuel injection.

As with the 250F, the success of the 300S could not be attributed to any single factor, but to an effective equilibrium between all its components.

In spite of those recognised attributes and the successes the car achieved in racing, the 300S suffered from competition with the 450S inside Maserati and soon fell into decline; it was also ill-served by the various calamities that hit the sports car category following a series of serious accidents, not least the 1957 De Portago debacle that spelt the end for the Mille Miglia. Regardless, this sports car experienced another fortunate period, competing in numerous United States races.

Technical specifications

ENGINE

Front, longitudinal, six cylinders in line
Bore and stroke: 84x90 mm
Cubic capacity: 2992.5 cc
Valve gear: twin overhead camshafts driven by gears
Number of valves: two per cylinder
Compression ratio: 9:1
Fuel feed: three Weber 42DCO3 (45 DCO3) carburettors
Ignition: double, with magnetos
Cooling: water
Lubrication: dry sump
Maximum power: 245 hp at 6200 rpm

TRANSMISSION

Rear wheel drive
Clutch: dry multi-disc
Gearbox: four forward speeds plus reverse in a single unit with
differential (from 1958, five speed)
Gear ratios: I) 0,46:1; II) 0,69:1; III) 0,83:1; IV) 1:1; R) 1.62:1
Axle ratio: 16/44 - 11/16

BODY

Two-seater roadster, in aluminium

CHASSIS AND MECHANICS

Chassis: trellis, elliptical-section tubes
Suspension: front – independent, upper and lower wishbones, coil
springs and Houdaille hydraulic dampers; rear –
De Dion axle, transverse leaf spring and Houdaille
hydraulic dampers
Brakes: hydraulically operated drums front and rear
Steering: worm and sector
Fuel tank: capacity 150 litres
Wheels: spoked, 5.00x16
Tyres: front 6.00x16, rear 6.50x16

DIMENSIONS AND WEIGHT

Wheelbase: 2310 mm
Track, front: 1300 mm
Track, rear: 1250 mm
Length: 4150 mm
Width: 1450 mm
Height: 980 mm
Dry weight: 780 kg

PERFORMANCE

Maximum speed: 180 mph

▽ *The long bonnet contrasts with the short nose, its large oval air intake and faired headlights.*

◁◁ *With its metal tonneau-cover reducing cockpit space, driving this 300S felt like being at the wheel of a single-seater.*

Chassis and engine numbers

Chassis and engine 3051 *(1955):* Briggs Cunningham, USA, for Bill Lloyd

Chassis and engine 3052 *(1955):* Briggs Cunningham, USA

Chassis and engine 3053 *(1955):* Briggs Cunningham, USA, for Bill Spear

Chassis and engine 3054 *(1955):* Maserati works car

Chassis and engine 3055 *(1955):* Maserati works car

Chassis and engine 3056 *(1955):* Robert Jenni, Switzerland (became 3077 in 1958)

Chassis and engine 3057 *(1955):* Benoit Musy, Switzerland

Chassis and engine 3058 *(1955):* Tony Parravano, USA

Chassis and engine 3059 *(1955):* Maserati works car

Chassis and engine 3060 *(1955):* sold in the USA

Chassis and engine 3061 *(1955):* Baron Pottino, Palermo

Chassis and engine 3062 *(1956):* Maserati works car

Chassis and engine 3063 *(1956):* Franco Bordoni, Milan

Chassis and engine 3064 *(1956):* owner unknown

Chassis and engine 3065 *(1956):* Maserati works car

Chassis and engine 3066 *(1956):* Maserati works car

Chassis and engine 3067 *(1956):* owner unknown

Chassis and engine 3068 *(1956):* Maserati works car

Chassis and engine 3069 *(1956):* owner unknown

Chassis and engine 3070 *(1957):* owner unknown

Chassis and engine 3071 *(1957):* Maserati works car

Chassis and engine 3072 *(1957):* Maserati works car

Chassis and engine 3073 *(1957):* owner unknown

Chassis and engine 3074 *(1957):* owner unknown

Engine 3075 *(1957):* owner unknown

Chassis and engine 3076 *(1957):* owner unknown

Chassis and engine 3077 *(1958):* Scuderia Centro-Sud, Rome (ex-3056)

Engine 3078: owner unknown

Engine 3079: owner unknown

Chassis and engine 3080 *(1958):* Stirling Moss, Great Britain

Engine 3081: owner unknown

△ Giorgio Scarlatti at the start
of the 1957 Mille Miglia.
He came fourth overall and
third in the over 2000 sports
car class, behind the Ferraris
of Piero Taruffi and
Wolfgang von Trips.
(A. Sorlini – Giorgio Nada
Editore Archives).

▷ *27 May 1956: the Maserati 300S driven by Piero Taruffi, Harry Schell, Jean Behra and Stirling Moss won the Nürburgring 1000 Kilometres.*

420M "Eldorado"

(1958-1959)

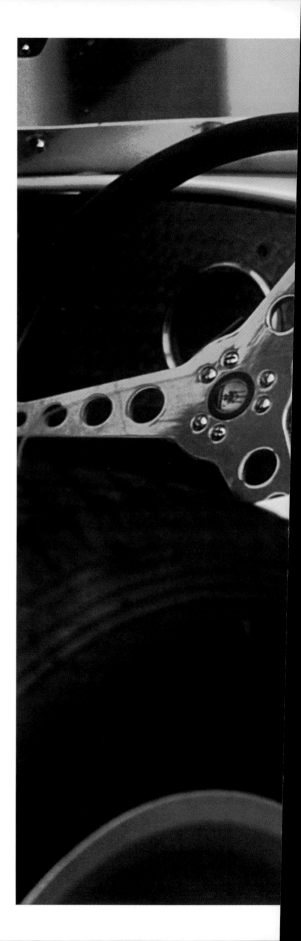

The Maserati 420M was a sort of comet that shot across motor racing's sky just twice. A unique newcomer to the Italian national competitive scene at the end of the Fifties, this Modena single-seater was white from stem to stern and had the name of its sponsor, the Eldorado ice-cream company as well as the manufacturer's cartoon cowboy trademark, painted prominently on its body: a dramatic break from Italy's usual red livery, which gave the world a foretaste of things to come - sponsorship. The genesis of the 420M is indelibly linked to the smiling face of Eldorado's cowboy trademark, known to millions of Italians to whom ice-cream is synonymous with summer, but the roots of this project and the car's brief excursion into the world of motor racing reached deep down into Maserati's history.

To begin with, the chassis of the 420M/58 was derived from the tubular structure of the 250F, while the engine was a re-elaboration of the 450S' V8 power plant, but with a cubic capacity of 4190.4 cc. The new power unit, obtained by reducing its original stroke to 75.8 mm, developed 410 hp at 8000 rpm while the engine of the second version of the car, designated the 420M/59 and earmarked for the Indianapolis 500, put out 450 hp at 7200 rpm.

Building a single-seater to compete in just two races could seem a rather hazardous affair, but one could also deduce from the situation that Maserati's real objective was to take part in the battle between the two opposing design schools of the old continent and the new. The "Eldorado" 420M/58 was, therefore, built in line with the technology necessary to race on the tracks of America.

The engine was offset by 9 cm to the longitudinal axis of the car, with the drive shaft running along the left side of the

continued on page 147

◁ The front end of the 420M shows its Maserati 250F Formula One single-seater parentage. Note the large air intake on the bonnet.

▷ On the left, concealed beneath metal faring riveted to the body, is the 30-litre engine oil reservoir.

continued from page 144

seat. The gearbox, with just two speeds of which first was only used to start a race, was in the rear axle, which had no differential.

An in-depth study of weight distribution was at the heart of the "Eldorado" project. The information revealed by that investigation was also the basis of the lightweight aluminium body by Medardo Fantuzzi, who conceived it with the intention of containing the car's weight, which worked out to be a mere 758 kg.

The track debut of the 420M/58 did not take place in America: on 29 June 1958, the "Eldorado" was on the grid for the 500 Miles of Monza, a race in which European and American single-seaters competed against each other.

The driver was one of the men of the moment and very much at home at Maserati: Stirling Moss. With an average qualifying speed of 164 mph, the white car started in 11th position, way down on pole sitter Luigi Musso's 170.7 mph in the 4.1-litre Ferrari. In the race's three heats, Moss came fourth in the first, the Premio Esso and fifth in the Premio Mobil. But during the third heat, the Premio Shell, the steering broke: the car flew off the track at 162 mph and crashed, a fortunate Moss eventually emerging uninjured from

continued on page 150

continued from page 147

the wreckage. But high speed crash or not, at the end of Premio Shell the "Eldorado" had still come seventh overall, with an aggregate of the three times it had set during the three heats.

In spite of the disappointing Monza performance, Gino Zanetti, owner of Eldorado, insisted on entering the car for the 1959 Indianapolis 500, for which it was modified, resulting in the abandonment of, among other things, the rear stabilising fin. With the intention of improving weight distribution, the 30-litre oil reservoir was moved to the left, outside the car's body.

Another high-speed gear was added, which acted as the reducer for the existing one. But the revised 420M/59, which was given a new red livery with its sponsors' name painted in white, soon became the victim of irresolvable carburetion problems, attributable to the large quantity of alcohol used in American fuel: as a result Ralph Liguori, the designated driver of the car at Indy, was unable to qualify it for the race.

So the 420M/59 returned to Italy and, stored away for more than 30 years, was restored by Maserati three decades later to its '58 livery and configuration, except that it retained the 1959 chassis modifications. Today, the car is a valuable survivor of motor racing history and part of a private collection: it still bursts into its unmistakable engine roar on occasions, usually at the more important events celebrating the glorious of the House of the Trident.

△ *The many air vents on the car's body contribute to evacuating the considerable heat generated by the engine and rear brake drums.*

▷▷ *The induction trumpets of the four Weber 46IDM carburettors stand proud between the two banks of the 4190.4 cc V8 engine, which develops up to 410 hp at 8000 rpm.*

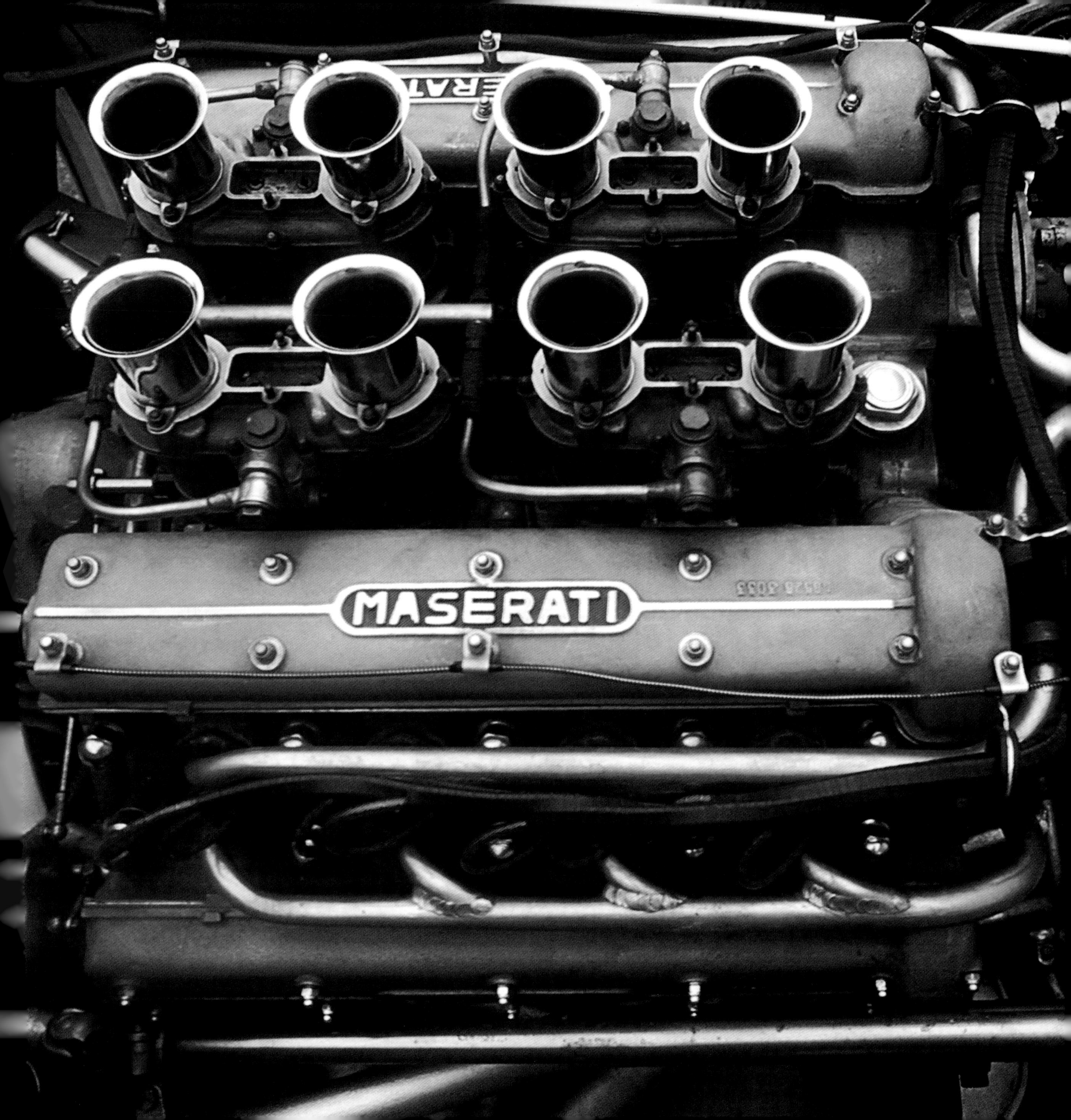
MASERATI

Technical specifications

ENGINE

Front, longitudinal, V8 at 90°
Bore and stroke: 93.8x75.8 mm
Cubic capacity: 4190.4 cc
Valve gear: twin overhead camshafts per cylinder bank
Number of valves: two per cylinder
Compression ratio: 12.5:1
Fuel feed: four Weber 46IDM carburettors
Ignition: double, with magnetos
Cooling: water
Lubrication: dry sump
Maximum power: 410 hp at 8000 rpm

TRANSMISSION

Rear wheel drive
Clutch: dry multi-disc
Gearbox: two forward speed plus reverse
Gear ratios: I) 14.2:1; II) 20.26:1
Axle ratio: 11/34

BODY

Single-seater, in aluminium

CHASSIS AND MECHANICS

Chassis: tubular, trellis structure
Suspension: front – independent, upper and lower wishbones, coil
spring and hydraulic dampers; rear – De Dion axle,
transverse semi-elliptic leaf spring and hydraulic dampers
Brakes: hydraulically operated drums front and rear
Steering: worm and sector
Fuel tank: capacity 250 litres
Wheels: light alloy
Tyres: front 7.60x16 . 8.00x16; rear 8.00x18

DIMENSIONS AND WEIGHT

Wheelbase: 2400 mm
Track, front: 1300 mm
Track, rear: 1250 mm
Length: 4800 mm
Width: 1200 mm
Height: 1100 mm
Dry weight: 758 kg

PERFORMANCE

Maximum speed: 218 mph

△ The cockpit of the 420M is more generous than those of the day's Formula One cars. Under the gear lever is a red leather pad on which the driver can lean his left leg. The dashboard hosts the traditional blue-dialled Maserati instruments, partially hidden by the large-diameter steering wheel with its three spokes perforated for weight saving and its wooden rim.

The small bonnet handle is particularly elegant and seems almost an affectation on such a car, chromed and with weight-saving perforations, an element that was common to many Maseratis.

The two exhaust terminals blow away from the car, so as not to overheat the large Firestone 8.00x18 rear tyres.

The rear view mirror is fixed to the left of the cockpit. Note the smooth flow between the body of the car and the windscreen.

The five rear air vents diminish in size towards the tail, their job to dissipate heat generated by the rear axle.

Chassis and engine number

Chassis and engine 4203 *(1958):* Maserati works car, updated in 1959

▽ The first Maserati 420M Eldorado in 1958, chassis number 4203, photographed in the Monza pits before the start of the 500 Miles race. Stirling Moss went off in the third heat with broken steering but, fortunately, was uninjured. He still finished seventh overall on aggregate.

△ The 420M/59 during a test session in
May 1959. The red body had lost its
faired, fin-shaped headrest that was a
feature of the 1958 car. The modification
was made to reduce the car's sensitivity to
cross wind at Indianapolis.

Tipo 61 "Birdcage"

(1959-1961)

An extremely complicated trelliswork of tubes that fascinated the great Stirling Moss, among others. In fact it was he who personally encouraged the development of the Tipo 61, with its three-litre engine. The big sister of the Tipo 60, with which Moss scored many victories and the chassis of which he considered exceptional, was based on the smaller-engined car's unique chassis and its magisterially intertwined small-gauge metal tubes, a structural concept which guaranteed the Maserati barchetta remarkable torsional resistance and lightness. And it is because of that structure that the men who worked on the Tipo 60 invented the car's nicknames, "Birdcage" and "Maserati Spaghetti", the first of which became even more famous than the car's official Tipo 61 designation. An evolution of the Tipo 60 was dictated by commercial need: the North American market was extremely interested in a three-litre sports car, so it was not by chance that all 17 of the Tipo 61s built by Maserati were sold in the USA. The commercial success of the Birdcage was, however, based on the fine reputation the car had established with its numerous race wins and the re-born confidence in the air at Maserati: the company had just emerged from bankruptcy, and the consequent economic adversity.

The "Birdcage" story began on the wave of success enjoyed by the 3500 GT, which was selling well in the sports road car sector. At the time, Maserati engineer Giulio Alfieri designed two new four-cylinder engines with twin overhead

continued on page 161

◁ *The Drogo body also encompasses the car's lower area, in which there are numerous air vents.*

▷ *The rear hood accommodates the characteristic Maserati aluminium fuel cap of a tank with a 120 litre capacity.*

continued from page 158

camshafts; the first to be built was a 1990 cc unit, which put out 200 hp at 7800 rpm. It was installed in a barchetta that was traditional as far as its mechanics were concerned, but had an extremely original chassis, made up of about 200 small-diameter tubes woven into an intricate weft: the car's engine was inclined at 45° to its longitudinal axis. This particular arrangement was adopted to lower the centre of gravity of the "Birdcage" and also meant the car could be given a more streamlined nose profile. Positioning the engine behind the front axle contributed to better weight distribution, guaranteeing notable road holding. To the same end, the gearbox and differential were made as a single unit to increase load on the rear axle and to better put down the power generated by the engine.

The "skin" for this singular chassis and its lowered engine was a tight-fitting body with wings that almost wrapped themselves around the wheels and tyres, which were not far from contact with the body; this permitted the adoption of an exceptionally low bonnet profile. The body was built by Gentilini and Allegretti of Modena and the various aluminium panels were shaped so as not to completely cover the interlaced chassis tubing, part of which could easily be seen protruding from under the windscreen in front of the driver. Deliberately pared down to save weight, when the new barchetta presented itself at races it's immediately

became highly competitive, to the point that it stupefied many drivers. Among them was Stirling Moss who, attracted to the exceptional roadholding of the "Birdcage" Maserati, decided to drive the car, winning an international race first time out, the Delamare-Deboutville Cup at Rouen, France, in July 1959. By transplanting the bigger 2890.3 cc engine into the light body of the Tipo 60 at the end of 1959, the House of the Trident created the new Maserati "Birdcage" Tipo 61. A fearsome weapon that became a great success in America by winning numerous races but which, more than anything, returned Maserati to victory in the prestigious World Constructors' Championship in Europe: the car won the Nürburgring 1000 Kilometres driven by Stirling Moss and Dan Gurney. The same car, chassis number 2472, driven by Lucky Casner of Team Camoradi, was involved in a serious accident during a race at Pescara in 1961: an accident that required the complete reconstruction of the car by the factory, after which Carrozzeria Drogo re-built the body. The "Birdcage" was given a new rear axle with independent rear suspension in

continued on page 167

▽ *The slender, rectangular air intake extended along the entire front section of the car. Along the right flank are air vents to dissipate heat from the engine exhaust.*

△ The prominent, low front end
is distinguished by the large,
faired light cluster and the
low, slim air intake. Those are
the details that made the Tipo
61 stand out as one of the
House of the Trident's most
unusual and interesting
barchettas.

continued from page 162

place of the original De Dion axle and was lengthened to accommodate a bigger fuel tank in the back end. Extending the tail meant a further re-dimensioning of the frontal area to ensure a balanced distribution of weight and aerodynamics that, as can be noted from this chapter's photographs of Tipo 61 chassis number 2472, was a major digression from the classical Tipo 61. This car acquired the informal designation CDM, from the initials of Cavalieri, creator of the body, Drogo, and the M of Maserati.

With the "Birdcage", Maserati returned to health after a period of economic ups and downs that also limited works participation in racing.

But with the evolution of the car into the Tipo 63 and 64, it was marching towards a brand new trend, the switch from front to rear engines.

△ *A curious and unusual shape for an air vent, found on the Tipo 61's left rear wing.*

◁ *The 4.50x16 spoked Rudge wheels were simple but elegant, harmonising well with the spontaneous lines of the car.*

▷ *The purposeful design of the body by Drogo found confirmation in the sloping tail and the low-profile of the vents beneath the door.*

Technical specifications

ENGINE

Front, longitudinal, four cylinders in line
Bore and stroke: 100x92 mm
Cubic capacity: 2890 cc
Valve gear: twin overhead camshafts driven by gears
Number of valves: two per cylinder
Compression ratio: 9.8:1
Fuel feed: two Weber 45DCO3 carburettors
Ignition: double, with distributors
Cooling: water
Lubrication: dry sump
Maximum power: 250 hp at 7000 rpm

TRANSMISSION

Rear wheel drive
Clutch: dry multi-disc
Gearbox: five speeds plus reverse
Gear ratios: I) 14.3:1; II) 15.25:1; III) 19.25:1; IV) 19.21:1; V) 22.22:1;
R) 1.62:1
Axle ratio: 43/17

BODY

Two-seater roadster, in aluminium

CHASSIS AND MECHANICS

Chassis: tubular, trellis structure
Suspension: front – independent, upper and lower wishbones, coil
springs and hydraulic telescopic dampers; rear – De Dion
axle, transverse semi-elliptic leaf spring and hydraulic
telescopic dampers
Brakes: hydraulically operated drums front and rear
Steering: rack and pinion
Fuel tank: capacity 120 litres
Wheels: spoked, 4.50x16
Tyres: front 5.50x16, rear 6.00x16

DIMENSIONS AND WEIGHT

Wheelbase: 2200 mm
Track, front: 1250 mm
Track, rear: 1200 mm
Length: 3800 mm
Width: 1500 mm
Height: 900 mm
Dry weight: 585 kg

PERFORMANCE

Maximum speed: 177 mph

The four-cylinder in-line power unit fed by two twin-choke Weber 45DCO3 carburettors.

△ The essential cockpit with wrap-around seats; in the foreground is the gear lever, for this example with a four-speed gate instead of five.

Chassis and engine numbers

Chassis and engine 2451 *(1959):* Team Camoradi, USA

Chassis and engine 2452 *(1959):* Joe Lubin, USA, for Bob Drake

Chassis and engine 2453 *(1959):* Edwin Martin, USA

Chassis and engine 2454 *(1959):* Loyal Katskee, USA

Chassis and engine 2455 *(1959):* Mike Garber, USA, for Guston Andrey

Chassis and engine 2456 *(1960):* Jack Hinkle, USA

Chassis and engine 2457 *(1959):* Dave Causey, USA

Chassis and engine 2458 *(1960):* Team Camoradi, USA

Chassis and engine 2459 *(1960):* Briggs Cunningham, USA,
for Walt Hansgen

Chassis and engine 2461 *(1960):* Team Camoradi, USA

Chassis and engine 2463 *(1960):* Hall-Shelby Inc., USA, for Jim Hall

Chassis and engine 2464 *(1960):* Team Camoradi, USA

Chassis and engine 2467 *(1960):* Frank Harrison, USA

Chassis and engine 2469 *(1960):* Harry Finer, USA

Chassis and engine 2470 *(1960):* Jack Hinkle, USA

Chassis and engine 2471 *(1960):* Hall-Shelby Inc., USA,
for Roger Penske

Chassis and engine 2472 *(1960):* Team Camoradi, USA

▽ Stirling Moss winning the
1960 Grand Prix of Cuba in a
Scuderia Camoradi Maserati
Tipo 61 Birdcage.

BARCHETTA
(1992)

Unveiled on 14 December 1991 to a small circle of enthusiastic clients and a number of selected journalists, the Maserati Barchetta made its debut in society according to the best traditions of the Trident: other Maserati new car presentations had been made on that date over the years. It was Maserati's hope and intention that, like the legendary A6GCS before it, the new barchetta would revive the fortunes of the House of the Trident through its involvement in racing. But the small number of cars produced – only 15 were sold, at a price of Lit 148 million each (about 12000 US $) and the car's subsequent bleak motor racing future relegated it to the lesser status of a collectors' item.

The potentially original idea of Alejandro De Tomaso, then Maserati's was to enable all Barchetta owners, strictly amateur drivers, to compete in a single marque championship of six races especially conceived for them, in which the manufacturer would rigorously ensure the parity of each car. That would have been possible by simply imposing a mono-tyre on the series, and substituting the engine management system of every car before the start of each race with another fitted by Maserati technicians, so as to avoid possible tampering to improve performance.

An interesting idea that, unfortunately, could only be put into practice for just a short period and a handful of races: the championship was negatively affected by a lack of competitors.

The Barchetta made its first track appearance at Monza, where the late Michele Alboreto covered a number of laps at a rapid pace, enthusing those attending by giving them

continued on page 177

◁ The three large black vents, through which front radiator heat is dissipated, help to give the Barchetta's front end an aggressive look.

continued from page 174

a glimpse of the car's notable potential. The Barchetta's technical pedigree said it all: a V6 bi-turbo engine, derived from the grand touring road car, which developed 315 hp at 7200 rpm, and a dry weight of 775 kg, which gave the Barchetta a power to weight ratio of 2.46 kg/hp and a maximum speed of around 186 mph.

The considerable care taken over the design of the chassis and suspension system put the Barchetta at the top of the sports car category of the period, with greater attention paid to its appearance and build quality, compared to its competitors. The carbon fibre body displayed an elegant aggressiveness; the air intakes and vents were well located and shaped to exploit, at the aesthetic level, the sporting image of the car.

Internally, Maserati preferred sobriety with a touch of added value from the simple, white-dialled instruments and tartan covered seats.

The chassis, the car's strong point, was built of a single beam structure in aluminium, with strengthening panels in

▷ Close together and easily legible, the cluster of white-dialled instruments, the largest of which is the central tachometer.

composite material; the cockpit was fixed to that structure to provide further rigidity.

The engine was anchored to an auxiliary chassis in light alloy; it was a 90° V6 with twin turbos, twin overhead cams-hafts for each cylinder bank and four valves per cylinder, all helping to develop a maximum torque of 40 kg/m at 4,500 revolutions per minute.

The suspension system was composed of upper and lower wishbones anchored to the central, light alloy mono-beam: there was a "push rod" for the front suspension and a "pull rod" for the rear. The petrol tank, made in flame retardant

▽ *The rear end of the Maserati Barchetta is square shaped; a sizeable wing increases downforce on the rear axle and the two recesses in the lower tail accommodate the exhaust terminals.*

▽ The front axle is in light alloy and fixed to a single beam, aluminium and composite materials chassis. The front suspension has an upper quadrilateral lay-out and large springs, similar to a Formula One car.

rubber, was inside the central beam. All this applied technology had an extremely positive effect on roadholding and stability, enabling the Maserati Barchetta to give an excellent account of itself on the track.

It is a great shame that the car was unable to look forward to a bright racing future, but it should be said that, during the year in which it was built, the House of the Trident was, once again, experiencing a difficult financial situation.

Even the winning image and notable potential of a car like the hi-tech Barchetta could not induce a significant number of clients to bring the factory's expectations to life.

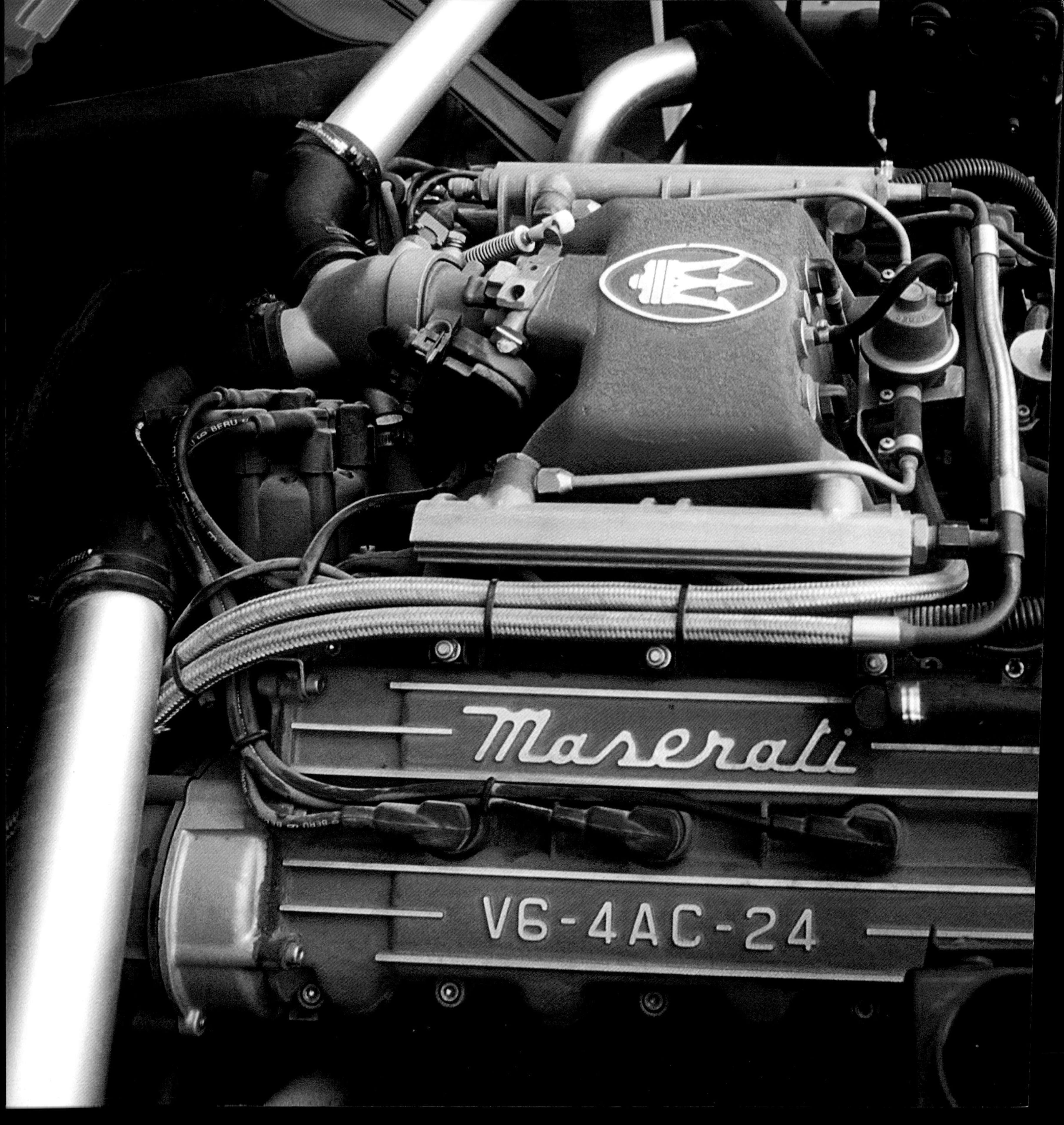
Maserati
V6-4AC-24

Technical specifications

ENGINE

Centre-rear, longitudinal, 90° V6

Bore and stroke: 82x63 mm

Cubic capacity: 1996 cc

Valve gear: twin overhead camshafts per cylinder bank

Number of valves: four per cylinder

Compression ratio: 9:1

Fuel feed: electronic injection, twin turbo

Ignition: electronic

Cooling: water (front radiator)

Lubrication: dry pump

Maximum power: 315 hp at 7,200 rpm

Maximum torque: 40 kg/m at 4,500rpm

TRANSMISSION

Rear wheel drive

Clutch: dry multi-disc

Gearbox: six forward speeds plus reverse

Gear ratios: I) 3,5:1; II) 1,89:1; III) 1,23:1; IV) 0,87:1; V) 0,67:1;
VI) 0,56:1; R) 3,62:1

Axle ratio: 3,85/1,13

BODY

Roadster, two-seater, composite

CHASSIS AND MECHANICS

Chassis: central beam in aluminium, reinforced with composite material

Suspension: independent front and rear, upper and lower wishbones,
coil springs and hydraulic telescopic dampers

Brakes: hydraulically operated discs front and rear

Steering: rack and pinion

Fuel tank: capacity 100 litres

Wheels: 17 inch

Tyres: front 235/45 ZR 17; rear 335/35 ZR 17

DIMENSIONS AND WEIGHT

Wheelbase: 2600 mm

Track, front: 1610 mm

Track, rear: 1580 mm

Length: 4050 mm

Width: 1965 mm

Height: 845 mm

Dry weight: 775 kg

PERFORMANCE

Maximum speed: 186 mph

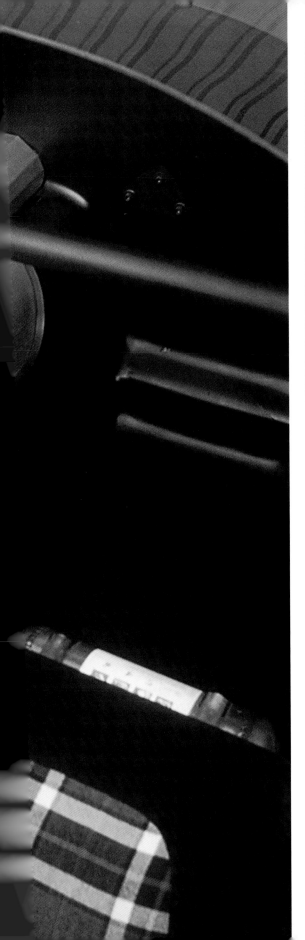

△ Once the front and rear
hoods have been removed,
the Barchetta reveals its
racing lineage. Note the
robust roll bar that protects
the driver.

◁ The cockpit is austere but
functional, almost incorporated
in the sides of the central
beam chassis. Note the
instruments set into a
transverse dash and the long
gearbox linkage.

Chassis numbers

Chassis 92LLC *(1992)*
Chassis 92LLD *(1992)*
Chassis 92LLE *(1992)*
Chassis 92LLF *(1992)*
Chassis 92LLG *(1992)*
Chassis 92LLH *(1992)*
Chassis 92LLI *(1992)*
Chassis 92LAL *(1992)*
Chassis 92LAA *(1992)*
Chassis 92LAB *(1992)*
Chassis 92LAC *(1992)*
Chassis 92LAD *(1992)*
Chassis 92LAE *(1992)*
Chassis 92LAF *(1992)*
Chassis 92LAG *(1992)*

▷ Track debut. The Maserati Barchetta lapping Monza for the first time on 6 september 1992, driven by the late Michele Alboreto.

Printed by
Bolis Poligrafiche SpA
Bergamo, Italy
August 2001